SAUCES of
INSPIRATION

SAUCES of INSPIRATION

Fresh + Modern Recipes

With Hundreds of Ideas for Elevating Everyday Dishes

Vanessa Seder

Photographs by Stacey Cramp

KYLE
BOOKS

To Katia, our miracle daughter who has brought us so much joy in life. One day when your palate expands beyond PB&J and buttered noodles, perhaps you'll enjoy some of these sauces and recipes.

An Hachette UK Company
www.hachette.co.uk

First published in Great Britain in 2017 by Kyle Books, an imprint of Octopus Publishing Group Ltd
Carmelite House, 50 Victoria Embankment, London EC4Y 0DZ
www.octopusbooks.co.uk

This edition published in 2025

Text copyright © 2017, 2025 Vanessa Seder
Design copyright © 2017, 2025 Octopus Publishing Group Limited
Photographs © 2017, 2025 Stacey Cramp

Distributed in the US by Hachette Book Group,
1290 Avenue of the Americas, 4th and 5th Floors, New York, NY 10104

Distributed in Canada by Canadian Manda Group,
664 Annette St., Toronto, Ontario, Canada M6S 2C8

Vanessa Seder is hereby identified as the author of this work in accordance with Section 77 of the Copyright, Designs, and Patents Act 1988.

ISBN 978-1-8041-9302-0

A CIP catalogue record for this book is available from the British Library

Printed and bound in China

10 9 8 7 6 5 4 3 2 1

Editor: Christopher Steighner | Copy Editor: Sarah Scheffel
Cover Design: Isobel Platt | Interior Design: Jennifer S. Muller
Photographer: Stacey Cramp | Stylist: Vanessa Seder
Production: Nic Jones and Gemma John

FSC
www.fsc.org
MIX
Paper | Supporting
responsible forestry
FSC® C008047

Right: The Mother Ganache, page 148

Contents

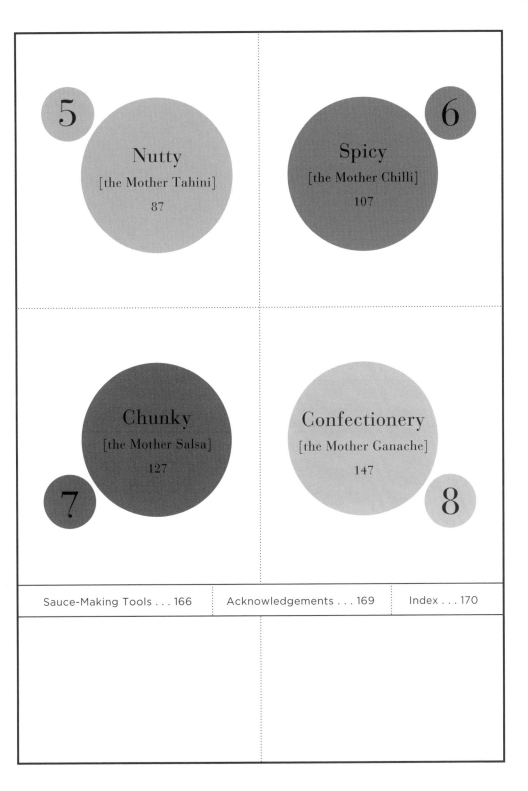

Woe to the cook whose sauces had no sting
Or who was unprepared in anything!
– Geoffrey Chaucer, *The Canterbury Tales*

Dip In

The concept for this cookbook – a collection of modern sauces with recipe pairing – was one that appealed to me for several reasons. First and foremost was the breadth of the canvas, so to speak. Sauces run the culinary gamut, spanning a multitude of cuisines, ingredients and uses. From marinades, dressings and dips to gravies, salsas and curries, they can and do appear with every course, from hors d'oeuvres through to dessert. Sweet or savoury, hot or cold, mild or spicy, smooth or chunky, sauces encompass an endless variety of components, flavour profiles, colours, aromas and textures.

Second, what better soapbox than a book of sauces to preach the merits of the international flavours and ingredients I love, while indulging my fascination with street foods from around the world? Plus it would allow me to draw on my culinary perspective as a born-and-bred Los Angelino and the wonderful Asian and Mexican influences prevalent throughout the city.

While I love French sauces, this book intentionally moves away from the heavy classic roux- and fond-based (page 82) sauces in favour of the light, the modern, the fresh. Think miso, pistachio, avocado and grapefruit. I have even developed my own 'mother sauces' – updated alternatives to the French classics (béchamel, velouté, espagnole, tomato and hollandaise). They're so called because each can form the base of countless variations and are designed as springboards – to act as 'sauces of inspiration' you might say). I've provided three to four spin-offs for each mother, but I hope you'll experiment and create your own variants.

You'll also find evidence within these pages of the decade I lived in New York City enjoying the unbelievable mixture of cuisines hidden throughout the five boroughs. Not that I had to go far for great food; my little Brooklyn neighbourhood had a wealth of really outstanding takeaway options ranging from Indian, Mexican and Thai to sushi, Middle Eastern and more. Many of these recipes were inspired by the desire to recreate the signature sauces that came with these meals and to 'decode' and reveal the secret and mysterious ingredients behind them.

Here's another secret: some sauces are hidden in plain sight. Even something as simple as seasoned olive oil can be a sauce of sorts. As you'll find, this book allows for a broad definition of what a sauce is, or can be.

I was drawn also to the idea of coming up with a featured recipe to pair with each sauce. As a chef instructor and recipe developer, I'm constantly thinking about mixing and matching flavours. However, these pairings presented a special challenge, since the purpose of any given sauce varies, depending on what it accompanies. Its role may be to enhance and intensify, to harmonize, or to provide a counterpoint to a specific dish. In some cases the sauce itself may be the star. Coming up with pairings that 'worked' with each of the 65 sauces forced me to stretch my culinary muscles to their limits, requiring me to constantly refine and revise, and to draw on everything I've learned in my years of problem-solving in the kitchen.

Last but not least, as a busy working mum, I'm hyper-conscious of time and budgetary constraints, and well aware of the need to make meals family friendly. While many of these recipes feature a range of ingredients, I've kept them as accessible and quick to prepare as possible and suggested substitutes for ingredients that might be tricky to track down, or challenging for cautious palates. Many of them were tested by my neighbours and based on their feedback I made adjustments to simplify or 'kid-ify' as needed. Storage information is provided for each sauce when appropriate, along with an 'Extra Credit' section with suggestions for alternative uses and repurposing.

To me the social aspect of eating and cooking is key. Delicious food transcends borders and language, and the sense of wellbeing it creates brings people together – families, friends, neighbours and strangers alike. I hope this book will inspire you to try some new flavours and ingredients, to play around and experiment with your own sauces, and to share them with the people in your life. And it never hurts to bring along a loaf of crusty bread for dipping.

Creamy

The Mother Mayo . . . 12

The Mother Mayo

Mayonnaise is an emulsino – a mixture of two liquids that don't really like being mixed. In this case the two liquids are egg yolks and oil. When left to their own devices, these two would stay separate, but by slowly whisking the oil into the yolks, you can trick the two into forming a silky smooth sauce. The science behind this is that one of the two liquids involved acts as an emulsifier. In the case of mayo, it is the lecithin found in the egg yolks that does the job.

Makes about 225g (8oz)

2 large egg yolks, at room temperature
1 tablespoon white wine vinegar
1 teaspoon Dijon mustard
150ml (5fl oz) rapeseed or grapeseed oil
Sea salt

1. Place the egg yolks, vinegar and mustard in the bowl of a food processor and pulse to combine. With the machine running, very, very slowly drizzle the oil into the bowl until the mixture begins to get thick and light.

2. Alternatively, you can make the mayo by hand (just be aware that this method is not as foolproof). In a large bowl, whisk together the egg yolks, vinegar and mustard. Very slowly drizzle in the olive oil while whisking quickly until the sauce becomes thick and light.

3. Season with salt to taste. The mayonnaise will last refrigerated in an airtight container for up to 3 days.

Mix It Up

Customize the mother sauce to your taste,
and to use in different ways.

Gochujang & Sesame Mayo

Stir in 2 teaspoons toasted sesame oil, 2½ teaspoons gochujang (fermented chilli paste) and 1 teaspoon toasted sesame seeds.

Smoky Tomato Mayo

Stir in 2 tablespoons tomato purée, 2 teaspoons smoked paprika and ½ teaspoon ground cumin.

Miso & Soy Mayo

Stir in 1 tablespoon sweet white miso, 1 teaspoon low-sodium soy sauce and 2 teaspoons mirin.

Lemon & Herb Mayo

Stir in 2 teaspoons lemon zest, 2 tablespoons lemon juice and 3 tablespoons herb of choice, such as chopped fresh parsley, chives, thyme, rosemary, chervil or tarragon.

Extra Credit

- Squiggle some gochujang or miso mayo on your **sushi**, or serve it with tempura or fried tofu.

- Spread the smoky tomato mayo on a **burger** instead of ketchup.

- Drizzle the miso and soy mayo over blanched **asparagus**.

- Serve the lemon and herb mayo with any **fried seafood**, or swipe artichoke leaves through it.

AVOCADO GREEN GODDESS

Green goddess dressing, a quintessentially California invention, is typically a mixture of fresh herbs, lemon, maybe a bit of anchovy and some creamy component. Rich and flavourful, green goddess is a simple way to add vivacity to healthy fare like poached chicken and steamed vegetables. However, it is also good on raw crunchy veggies. To make it even more California-centric, my green goddess uses avocado along with some soured cream for creaminess.

Makes about 225g (8oz)

65g (2¼oz) chopped avocado
55g (2oz) soured cream
3 tablespoons rice vinegar
2 teaspoons anchovy paste (optional)
1 teaspoon lemon zest
2 teaspoons fresh lemon juice
20g (¾oz) chopped fresh herbs,
such as flat-leaf parsley, tarragon,
basil and/or chives
Sea salt and freshly ground black pepper

Combine all ingredients in a food processor or high-powered blender and process or blend until smooth. Season to taste with salt and pepper. Use immediately or store refrigerated in an airtight container for up to 3 days.

Extra Credit

Spoon over fresh **spring greens** or butterhead lettuce; you need nothing more for a superb salad.

Drizzle the sauce over a fish, prawns (shrimp) or **lobster taco**.

Stir into shredded rotisserie chicken and place between 2 slices of bread with some baby spinach for a California riff on a **chicken salad sandwich**.

Blend with an extra avocado or two plus buttermilk to achieve a soupy consistency, then chill to create a refreshing **green summer soup**.

The Un-Crudités

Place 4 large eggs in a medium saucepan and add enough cold water to submerge the eggs by 5cm (2in). Bring to the boil over a high heat. Turn off the heat, cover and let steam for 4 minutes. Transfer the eggs to a large bowl of ice water until cool to the touch, then set the eggs aside.

Bring a large pot of heavily salted water to the boil over a high heat. Ready a large bowl of ice water for shocking the vegetables, replacing ice as needed. Scoop 55g (2oz) of the avocado green goddess into a ramekin on each of four plates and set aside.

Cut 350g (12oz) broccoli and 350g (12oz) cauliflower into 7.5cm (3in) florets and add to the boiling water. Cook until crisp tender, about 4 minutes, then immediately plunge the florets into the ice water. Drain in a colander and then divide among the plates. Trim 350g (12oz) asparagus spears, add to the boiling water and cook until crisp tender, about 2 minutes. Plunge them into the ice water, drain in the colander and divide among the plates. Trim off the stem end of 280g (10oz) green beans, add to the boiling water and cook until crisp tender, about 4 minutes. Plunge them into the ice water, drain in the colander and divide among the plates.

Peel and halve the eggs and add 2 halves to each of the plates. Sprinkle with sea salt and serve immediately. **Serves 4**

HORSERADISH CRÈME FRAÎCHE

This deceptively simple sauce contributes a creamy kick to whatever it encounters, elevating even the plainest platforms, such as a skinless chicken breast. I especially like the unexpected zing it brings to any form of potato. Try it as a topping for baked potatoes, stirred into mashed potatoes, or as an alternative to ketchup for fries. Crème fraîche provides a shortcut for sauces; it gives you that unctuous texture you crave in a cream sauce but without having to make a roux with flour and cream. I recommend fresh horseradish root if you can locate it. To prepare the root, peel first, then grate with a Microplane.

Makes about 285g (10oz)

215g (7½oz) crème fraîche
3 tablespoons grated fresh or jarred horseradish
2 tablespoons Dijon mustard
4 teaspoons fresh lemon juice
Sea salt and freshly ground black pepper

Stir together the crème fraîche, horseradish, mustard and lemon juice in a medium bowl. Season to taste with salt and pepper. Use immediately or store refrigerated in an airtight container for up to 3 days.

Extra Credit

Funnel the sauce into a squeezy bottle and use it on top of **hot dogs** or grilled sausages. It also cries out to be slathered on a roast beef sandwich.

Spoon a little on **canned sardines** or smoked oysters on sea salt crackers or saltines for a transcendent experience.

Add a dollop to **roasted beetroot** or on top of borscht.

For a **bagel brunch**, serve horseradish crème fraîche instead of cream cheese along with smoked fish.

16

Crostini with Rib-Eye and Greens

Preheat the oven to 200°C (400°F), Gas Mark 6. Cut 12 thin slices on a bias from a baguette. Place on a baking sheet and lightly brush with olive oil. Toast in the oven until lightly golden around the edges, about 10 minutes.

Heat a medium cast-iron or heavy-bottomed frying pan over a medium-high heat. Meanwhile, season a 350g (12oz) piece of beef rib-eye with salt and pepper.

When the pan is hot, coat the bottom of the pan with olive oil and add the rib-eye. Sear the steak without moving it until a brown crust forms, 3–5 minutes. Flip and continue to cook the steak for about 3 minutes for medium rare, or 5 minutes for medium.

Transfer to a board and let rest for about 5 minutes. Cut the rib-eye across the grain into 12 slices. Top each baguette slice with thinly sliced radishes, baby rocket (arugula), a slice of the steak and a dollop of horseradish crème fraîche. Serve immediately. **Serves 4**

DILL AND PRESERVED LEMON RÉMOULADE

Rémoulade, a traditional French mayo-based sauce, is generally used for dipping or dressing vegetables. In Cajun cuisine, rémoulade is pink, thanks to the addition of hot sauce or cayenne pepper. I like mine more mild and fresh tasting, via the addition of Moroccan preserved lemon and fresh dill, but if it's Mardi Gras or you're craving a jolt, add a couple of squirts of hot sauce.

A staple condiment of Moroccan cooking, preserved lemons could just as easily be called pickled lemons. Traditionally they are made by combining fresh lemons with large amounts of salt and lemon juice in a jar and letting the lemons pickle at room temperature. The pickling process usually takes several weeks or even longer. The peel becomes very soft and loses its pithy bitterness. Before use, many cooks wash off the salt and remove the membranes and seeds. I love preserved lemons so much I find myself eating them on their own, but they add an intense lemon flavour to any dish you choose, such as a classic tagine stew, a couscous salad or this rémoulade.

Makes about 285g (10oz)

70g (2½oz) soured cream
150g (5½oz) mayonnaise
2 tablespoons Dijon mustard
1 tablespoon finely chopped shallot
30g (1oz) chopped cornichons
10g (¼oz) chopped fresh dill
3 tablespoons chopped preserved lemon
Sea salt and freshly ground black pepper

Whisk together the soured cream, mayonnaise, mustard, shallot, cornichons, dill and preserved lemon in a medium bowl. Season to taste with salt and pepper. Use immediately or store refrigerated in an airtight container for up to 3 days.

Extra Credit

Rémoulade, especially with preserved lemons, calls out to be paired with **fish and chips** or any fried seafood.

Add some fresh lemon juice and olive oil to the mix and use as a creamy dressing over **raw baby kale**, spinach and rocket (arugula).

Toss with **roasted carrots** and chopped fresh mint for a zingy salad.

Serve with boiled and cooled **new** or **fingerling potatoes** for an easy starter.

Oyster Po' Boys

Drain 16 shucked oysters in a fine-mesh sieve. Whisk together 1 large egg and 3 tablespoons buttermilk in a medium bowl. Add the oysters to the bowl and gently toss to coat with the egg mixture.

In a separate shallow bowl, whisk together 150g (5½oz) finely ground polenta, 1½ teaspoons seafood seasoning, 30g (1oz) plain flour, 1 teaspoon salt and ½ teaspoon freshly ground black pepper.

Heat 2.5cm (1in) rapeseed oil in a large high-sided frying pan until it registers 180°C (350°F) on a deep-fry thermometer. Dip the oysters in the polenta mixture and then fry in batches in the oil until golden brown and crisp, 2–3 minutes per batch. Transfer with a slotted spoon to a kitchen paper-lined baking sheet.

Slice four 20cm (8in) rolls in half lengthways, toast them and spread some of the rémoulade on the bottom half of each. Top each with 4 oysters, shredded iceberg lettuce and shredded purple cabbage. Add the top halves of the rolls and serve immediately. **Serves 4**

NYC STREET MEAT SAUCE

Nothing evokes New York City street food like the ubiquitous white sauce dispensed from clear squirt bottles at food carts from Battery Park to the Bronx Zoo. I have fond memories of the day I was first introduced to it. A recent West Coast transplant, I was temping at a large law firm in midtown Manhattan and some coworkers invited me to join them for lunch. They took me to a small cart and as we inched closer to the front of the line, the fragrant aromas circling the air were nearly too much to take. My mouth was watering by the time I made it to the vendor. Unsure of what to order, I went with what looked like the popular choice: a simple platter of sizzling gyro meat sliced off a vertical spit, rice, salad and white sauce. The meat was so succulent and flavourful that I was instantly hooked. But the thing that really completed the meal was that white sauce. Not quite a dressing, not quite a dip, the sauce proves to be an excellent creamy foil for smoky foods off the grill. With this recipe, you can enjoy white sauce at home, eaten from a real plate instead of a Styrofoam container. Try it at your next barbecue.

Makes about 215g (7½oz)

150g (5½oz) full-fat Greek yogurt	In a medium bowl, whisk together the
115g (4oz) mayonnaise	yogurt, mayonnaise, 2 tablespoons water,
1 teaspoon sugar	the sugar, vinegar, lemon juice and sea
1 teaspoon white vinegar	salt until combined. Use immediately or
1 teaspoon fresh lemon juice	store refrigerated in an airtight container or
1 teaspoon sea salt	squeezy bottle for up to 1 week.

Extra Credit

● Add a bunch of chopped fresh herbs of any variety and call it an **'herb dip'** for French fries or potato crisps.

● Liven up the blandest of cooked **chicken breasts**: cook them under the grill for a minute with some crumbled feta and this sauce.

● For an easy side dish or veggie meal, top a roasted baked **sweet potato** with a few squirts of street meat sauce, some harissa sauce (page 109), fresh coriander (cilantro) and chopped almonds.

● Add a bunch of chopped herbs of any variety, a tablespoon more vinegar and 2 tablespoons olive oil to make a creamy salad dressing for a **spinach salad** with sliced beetroot and hard-boiled eggs.

Middle Eastern Lamb Meatballs on a Bed of Rice and Greens

Preheat the oven to 110°C (225°F), Gas Mark ¼. Soak 15g (½oz) breadcrumbs torn from stale bread in 2 tablespoons milk in a large bowl until the breadcrumbs absorb most of the milk, about 3 minutes. Add 550g (1lb 4oz) minced lamb, 1 large egg, lightly beaten, 10g (¼oz) chopped fresh parsley, 2 finely chopped garlic cloves, 1 teaspoon grated fresh ginger, ½ teaspoon ground cumin, 1 teaspoon ground sumac, 1 teaspoon sweet paprika, 1 teaspoon ras el hanout (Moroccan spice blend), ½ teaspoon ground coriander (cilantro), ¼ teaspoon ground cardamom, 1¾ teaspoons sea salt and ½ teaspoon freshly ground black pepper. Use your hands to mix well and shape into 16 meatballs about 4cm (1½in) in diameter.

Heat a medium cast-iron or heavy-bottomed frying pan over a medium-high heat. Add 1 tablespoon olive oil to the pan. Add half of the meatballs to the pan and cook, turning gently until all sides are browned and the meatballs are just cooked through, about 8 minutes. Transfer to a parchment-lined baking sheet and place in the oven to keep warm. Pour 1 more tablespoon olive oil into the pan and repeat the cooking with the remaining meatballs.

Divide cooked rice among four plates. Top with the meatballs and serve with a pile of chopped romaine lettuce. Drizzle all over with NYC street meat sauce and harissa sauce (page 109), if desired. Garnish with fresh mint and a lemon wedge. **Serves 4**

SALSA GOLF

You may recognize this recipe as the 'secret sauce' at old-school burger joints. But according to legend, its origins reach to Argentina. The story starts with Luis Federico Leloir, a Nobel laureate biochemist famous for his discovery and study of sugar nucleotides. Luis was something of a regular at a seaside golf resort, but he grew sick of the plain old mayo on the prawn (shrimp) cocktail it served. Drawing on his chemical genius, he requested that ketchup be mixed in. And so Salsa Golf was born. My interpretation includes a bit of roasted red pepper and pickle juice, and will add a creamy charge to any number of dishes, no research required.

Makes 150g (5½oz)

115g (4oz) mayonnaise
2 tablespoons ketchup
1 teaspoon fresh lemon juice
2 tablespoons chopped roasted red pepper
2 teaspoons pickle juice from a jar of gherkins or dill pickles
½ teaspoon onion powder
Sea salt

Place the mayonnaise, ketchup, lemon juice, roasted red pepper, pickle juice and onion powder in a food processor and process until smooth. Season to taste with salt.

- Replicate that carnival stand experience by serving some of this sauce on top of a hot dog or **sausage along with grilled peppers and onions.**

- Serve alongside fries or **hash browns.**

- Use salsa golf instead of mayo to make amped-up **devilled eggs.**

- Keep it old school and coat a hunk of chilled **iceberg lettuce** with this sauce, steakhouse style.

Lobster Louie Salad

Preheat the oven to 190°C (375°F), Gas Mark 5. Toss 100g (3½oz) of 2.5cm (1in) Italian or white bread cubes with 3 tablespoons melted unsalted butter, 1 teaspoon Old Bay or seafood seasoning and ¼ teaspoon salt. Spread the seasoned bread cubes out on a baking sheet and bake until golden brown and crispy, 8–10 minutes. Transfer the baking sheet to a wire rack to cool.

Divide 265g (9½oz) chopped Cos lettuce among four large bowls and top each bowl with 1 quartered hard-boiled egg, 35g (1¼oz) chopped celery, 2 tablespoons chopped celery leaves, 35g (1¼oz) chopped avocado, 35g (1¼oz) grated carrot, 45g (1½oz) halved small cherry tomatoes, 85g (3oz) cooked fresh lobster meat and the croutons. Drizzle with salsa golf. **Serves 4**

Special vs. Secret: McDonald's launched a new condiment in the 1970s, dubbing it *Special Sauce*. Not to be outdone, fast food rival Jack-in-the-Box unveiled its own take, subtly switching the name to *Secret Sauce*.

LIMEY MASALA

In the 1950s, many people emigrated from India to the UK and opened up restaurants. One evening at one such restaurant, a customer complained that his chicken tikka masala was too dry. Frustrated and insulted, the chef added a can of tomato soup and some soured cream. To his dismay, this odd hybrid masala became a hit. It is a dish hard not to love: creamy, rich and filled with flavour from all the spices. My version of masala sauce balances the sweetness of the tomato and richness of the cream with bright notes of fresh lime and lime zest – with nary a can of soup.

Makes about 350g (12oz)

3 tablespoons ghee or butter
60g (2¼oz) chopped white onion
2 teaspoons grated fresh ginger
2 garlic cloves, finely chopped
½ teaspoon ground cumin
½ teaspoon ground coriander (cilantro)
1 teaspoon garam masala (savoury Indian spice blend)
¼ teaspoon fenugreek seeds
2 tablespoons tomato purée
160g (5¾oz) crushed canned or finely chopped tomatoes
2 tablespoons lime zest
115ml (3¾fl oz) double cream
3 tablespoons full-fat Greek yogurt
1 tablespoon fresh lime juice
Sea salt and freshly ground black pepper

1. In a medium saucepan, melt the ghee over a medium-high heat. Add the onion and cook, stirring occasionally, until golden, about 6 minutes. Add the ginger and garlic and cook just until fragrant, about 30 seconds, then add the cumin, coriander, garam masala and fenugreek seeds. Stir to combine.

2. Stir in the tomato purée and cook, stirring constantly, until the tomato purée begins to caramelize, about 2 minutes. Add the tomatoes, lime zest and cream and bring to a simmer, stirring constantly, until the flavours develop, 2–3 minutes. Stir in the yogurt and lime juice. Season to taste with salt and pepper. Use immediately or store refrigerated in an airtight container for up to 3 days.

Extra Credit

Bake **salmon** in the sauce until it flakes easily. Or, for a vegetarian alternative, try it with extra-firm tofu.

For a creamy grain or rice topping, drain a can of **chickpeas** and cook with some limey masala with handfuls of fresh spinach until the spinach wilts.

Forget those omnipresent sticky-sweet **Swedish meatballs**. Instead drape cooked meatballs in this sauce and serve with toothpicks for your next party.

New Delhi-Style Chicken Legs

In a medium bowl, stir together 110g (4oz) full-fat Greek yogurt and 145g (5¼oz) cooled limey masala, 1 teaspoon ground cumin, 1 teaspoon ground coriander, 2 teaspoons salt and 1 teaspoon pepper. Use a knife to poke holes all over 4 bone-in skin-on chicken leg quarters with the thighs still attached (about 1.1kg/2lb 8oz total), then place them in a large resealable bag along with the sauce mixture. Remove air from the bag, seal and use your hands to press and move the bag around to coat the chicken legs in the marinade. Refrigerate for at least 2 hours or overnight.

Preheat the oven to 220°C (425°F), Gas Mark 7 with racks on the middle and upper levels. Place the chicken in a single layer in a 23 x 33cm (9 x 13in) roasting pan or baking dish. Spoon the remaining 215g (7½oz) limey masala over the chicken and use tongs to coat with the sauce. Roast on the middle rack until the juices run clear and the chicken has an internal temperature of 74°C (165°F), about 30 minutes.

Transfer the chicken to the upper rack and grill until browned in parts, about 5 minutes. Rest for about 10 minutes. Garnish with chopped white onion and coriander sprigs and serve with basmati rice and naan, if desired. **Serves 4**

FAUX AIOLI

Aioli has popped up on restaurant menus everywhere. It's irresistible, but if you want to make it the traditional Provençal way, you must use a mortar and pestle and include egg yolks. This widely divergent recipe skirts those items. Instead it's a simple sauce that brings together two indulgent favourites of mine: cream and tahini. Though you may think that adding cream to tahini, already rich unto itself, may seem akin to gilding the lily, each brings a different kind of richness. Plus I find that the cream and yogurt help balance any bitterness in the tahini. Some may fear using raw garlic, but take heart – this recipe doesn't call for much and it adds an intensity of flavour that you can't replicate with cooked or roasted garlic. This rich sauce is more spreadable than drizzly; if you want to thin it out, whisk in a couple of tablespoons of water. I like using it in place of mayo as a spread for sandwiches.

Makes about 225g (8oz)

55ml (2fl oz) tahini	Whisk together the tahini, lemon zest,
2 teaspoons lemon zest	yogurt, garlic and cream in a medium bowl.
110g (4oz) full-fat natural yogurt	Season to taste with salt. Use immediately
2 garlic cloves, minced	or store refrigerated in an airtight container
55ml (2fl oz) double cream	for up to 3 days.
Sea salt	

Extra Credit

- Roast a whole **cauliflower head**, then serve with this sauce on the side for a dramatic veggie main dish.

- Swirl into a bowl of **lentils** and serve with rice or couscous.

- Add a dollop of faux aioli to warm broccoli, cauliflower or **winter squash soup**.

- Smear onto toasted flatbread and fold thinly sliced roast beef or lamb on top for a **shawarma** of sorts.

26

Beetroot and Polenta Cakes

Follow the packet instructions to make plain coarse-grain polenta (you'll need 800g/1lb 12oz cooked). Let the polenta cool to room temperature, then transfer to a large bowl.

Add 135g (4¾oz) chopped roasted beetroot, 10g (¼oz) fresh chopped parsley, 1 teaspoon ground cumin,½ teaspoon ground coriander (cilantro), 2 teaspoons fresh lemon juice, 2 teaspoons honey,

1 large egg, 1½ teaspoons salt and ½ teaspoon freshly ground black pepper. Stir to combine and then form into 8 round cakes approximately 7.5cm (3in) in diameter.

Heat 2 tablespoons olive oil in a large cast-iron frying pan over a medium-high heat. Add half of the cakes and cook until golden brown, about 4 minutes per side. Repeat with the remaining cakes and more oil if needed. Transfer the cakes to a plate and dollop with the faux aioli. **Serves 4**

Tangy

The Mother Vinaigrette

Whipping up a vinaigrette is a snap. The difference between fresh and bottled is night and day, and you probably have most of the ingredients in your pantry already. Like mayo (page 12), vinaigrette is an emulsion of two liquids, but instead of oil and egg yolk, it is an emulsion of oil and vinegar. The secret is to slowly drizzle in the oil while whisking constantly to end up with a creamy and smooth texture. (Whisking, incidentally, is why even the most rotund chefs have muscular arms.) Most vinaigrettes will last up to one week. They're great served with just about any green salad or grilled vegetables. I store them in jars in my fridge (just shake before use), so they're ready to make meals a snap.

Makes about 75ml (2½fl oz)

1½ teaspoons Dijon mustard
1 tablespoon finely chopped shallot
2 tablespoons rice wine vinegar or white wine vinegar
50ml (2fl oz) extra virgin olive oil
Salt and freshly ground black pepper

1. In a medium bowl, whisk the mustard, shallot and vinegar together.

2. Very slowly drizzle in the olive oil while whisking constantly until emulsified. Season to taste with salt and pepper.

3. Alternatively, place the mustard, shallot, vinegar and olive oil in a jar and vigorously shake for 30 seconds–1 minute until combined. Season to taste with salt and pepper.

Mix It Up

Customize the mother sauce to your taste,
and to use in different ways.

Tomato & Basil Vinaigrette

Stir in 3 tablespoons finely chopped tomato, 1 teaspoon chopped fresh oregano and 1 tablespoon chopped fresh basil.

Parmesan & Almond Vinaigrette

Stir in 3 tablespoons freshly grated Parmesan cheese, 2 tablespoons finely chopped toasted almonds and 1 teaspoon chopped fresh thyme leaves.

Cucumber & Buttermilk Vinaigrette

Stir in 30g (1oz) grated peeled cucumber. Replace the vinegar with 3 tablespoons buttermilk and add 1 tablespoon chopped fresh dill.

Dulse & Sesame Vinaigrette

Stir in 1 tablespoon dulse seaweed flakes, 2 teaspoons toasted sesame seeds and 2 teaspoons toasted sesame oil.

Extra Credit

● Fill the hole of a **pitted avocado with poached prawns (shrimp)** and drizzle your choice of vinaigrette over the top.

● Forget the pats of butter; Parmesan almond vinaigrette will take **baked potatoes** to a whole new level.

● Drizzle the tomato basil variation over cubes of stale bread and let sit for about 20 minutes. Then toss in fresh mozzarella, basil and sliced tomato for an amped-up **panzanella salad**.

● Say goodbye to the powdered ranch mix that comes in a packet from the supermarket; use cucumber buttermilk vinaigrette as you would ranch dressing as a dip for carrots and/or **chicken wings**.

BENGALI SPICED YOGURT

When I was growing up in LA, my family often went to a local Indian restaurant. The food was delicious and I wanted so badly to enjoy it, but the spice level was often too much for my young palate. I felt like a wimpy kid. But then I discovered the secret power of the yogurt sauces on the side. First, there was the mild raita, filled with cooling cucumbers, and then there was the coriander (cilantro) and yogurt chutney. My version is an amalgam of the two but substitutes mint for the cucumbers and coriander. It makes a flavourful yet cooling counterpart to any dish that's laced with chilli heat. With this alongside your plate, you'll never again have to worry about wimping out in the face of spicy foods.

Makes 325g (11½oz)

2 teaspoons mustard seeds
1 teaspoon cumin seeds
325g (11½oz) full-fat natural yogurt
1 teaspoon grated fresh ginger
1 tablespoon finely chopped shallot
10g (¼oz) chopped fresh mint
Sea salt

Place the mustard and cumin seeds in a medium frying pan and heat over a medium heat, stirring constantly until toasted, about 3 minutes. Transfer to a medium bowl. Add the yogurt and the rest of the ingredients, stir to combine and season with salt to taste.

Toasting spices in a dry frying pan or with a bit of oil intensifies their flavour. Just go easy – once the aroma hits your nose, they're done. Add to your dish or grind as needed.

Extra Credit

- Try this spiced yogurt on turkey or **lamb burgers**. Or for a vegetarian option, fried aubergine (eggplant) cutlets.

- Tame the spice of grilled **merguez sausages** with this cooling sauce, slathered on flatbread.

- Top a bowl full of rocket (arugula) and tomatoes with a piece of **roasted salmon**. Spoon a dollop of the sauce onto the salmon for a healthy and flavourful lunch.

- Drizzle over a **grain bowl** – perhaps barley with roasted butternut squash.

Roasted Sweet Potato Wedges

Preheat the oven to 220°C (425°F), Gas Mark 7. Scrub 2 large sweet potatoes (about 900g/2lb) and slice lengthways into 1cm (½in) thick wedges.

Place in a large bowl and toss with 2 tablespoons extra virgin olive oil, 2 tablespoons brown sugar, 1 teaspoon ground cumin, ½ teaspoon ground coriander, 1 teaspoon salt and ½ teaspoon black pepper.

Spread out on a parchment-lined baking sheet and roast, flipping once during the cooking, until golden brown and crisp in parts, 40–45 minutes.

Transfer to a serving dish and drizzle with Bengali spiced yogurt. Garnish with finely chopped parsley or coriander . Serve immediately. **Serves 4**

MISO AND LIME DRESSING

A thick fermented paste commonly made using soya beans (though it can be made with other grains or pulses such as barley or chickpeas), miso is generally associated only with the ubiquitous soup that bears its name. That's a shame, because its uses are many. For instance, in Japan it's often used as a glaze for cooked fish or aubergine (eggplant); I even put it in caramel (page 162). What makes miso a standout is that it adds umami to anything it touches. Umami describes that rich and savoury flavour that you get from things like Parmesan, beef stock or mushrooms. This recipe adds a tangy citrus jolt to the mild, sweet and salty flavour miso provides. Try it first with a mild soya bean miso and then experiment with other types of miso if you like; I keep an arsenal close by at all times.

Makes about 100ml (3½fl oz)

3 tablespoons sweet white miso
2 teaspoons minced garlic
1 tablespoon agave nectar or honey
1 tablespoon sesame oil
3 tablespoons fresh lime juice
1 tablespoon low-sodium soy sauce

In a medium bowl, whisk together the miso, garlic, agave, sesame oil, lime juice, soy sauce and 3 tablespoons water. Use immediately or store refrigerated in an airtight container for up to 1 week.

Extra Credit

- Blanch **green beans** or broccoli florets and toss with the dressing. Top with sesame seeds. This side is good warm or at room temperature.

- Serve seared **tuna steak** atop salad greens with the dressing drizzled over all.

- Do a Japanese-style **potato salad** for your next picnic: toss boiled new or fingerling potatoes while still warm with miso and lime dressing, then with chopped spring onions.

- Thread extra-firm **tofu cubes** and 5cm (2in) pieces of spring onions onto kebab sticks. Season with salt, brush with toasted sesame oil and grill. Drizzle with the dressing.

Seared Sea Scallops with Microgreens Salad

Remove the side muscle from 12 dry sea scallops if you find any still attached. Season the scallops to taste with salt and pepper.

In a small bowl, toss 100g (3½oz) microgreens and 3 chopped radishes with 3 tablespoons miso and lime dressing and set aside.

Heat a cast-iron griddle or frying pan over a medium-high heat. Add 1 tablespoon olive oil and the scallops to the pan and cook until golden brown and seared on the outside and just opaque on the inside, about 2 minutes per side.

Divide the scallops among four plates and top each with a small mound of salad. Drizzle the scallops with additional dressing, if desired. Serve immediately. **Serves 4**

XANADU PEPPER DREAM

A shiny and sweet sauce, Xanadu pepper dream was inspired by the slightly gummy, translucent red Thai sweet chilli sauce I've found in local Southeast Asian supermarkets. I've always loved the addictive flavour, but wondered about the preservatives in the ingredients. So I decided to see if I could create a homemade facsimile. This version has a brighter flavour due in part to the fresh peppers. Its unctuous texture and attractive sheen come from a bit of cornflour. From wontons to egg rolls, it's great with anything hot, crisp and fried.

Makes about 185g (6½oz)

3 garlic cloves, crushed
2 teaspoons chopped fresh Fresno or red jalapeño chilli
55g (2oz) chopped red pepper
90ml (6 tablespoons) rice vinegar
45g (1½oz) sugar
2 teaspoons cornflour
Sea salt

1. Place the garlic, chilli and red pepper in a food processor and pulse, scraping down the bowl if necessary, until finely chopped.

2. Combine 90ml (6 tablespoons) water, the vinegar and sugar in a saucepan and bring to the boil over a high heat, 2–3 minutes. Stir in the garlic and chilli mixture. Reduce to medium-low heat and simmer until the garlic is soft, about 4 minutes.

3. In a small bowl, whisk the cornflour and 2 teaspoons water until dissolved.

4. Return the sauce to the boil over a medium heat. Whisk in the cornflour and water mixture and continue to cook and stir until the sauce thickens. Continue to boil and stir for another 2–3 minutes. Season to taste with salt. Store refrigerated in an airtight container for up to 3 weeks.

Extra Credit

● Dab a stripe of sauce across a lettuce leaf and throw some **shredded cabbage**, carrots, spring onions and peanuts on top. Roll up and eat.

● Toss store-bought (or homemade) **fried chicken pieces** in the sauce for a sweet and crunchy treat.

Crisp Roasted Cabbage and Bacon

Preheat the oven to 200°C (400°F), Gas Mark 6. Line a rimmed baking sheet with baking parchment and lay 5 slices of bacon on it. Cook until the bacon is golden brown and crisp, 18–20 minutes. Transfer the bacon to a board and coarsely chop, reserving the bacon fat on the baking sheet.

Increase the oven temperature to 220°C (425°F), Gas Mark 7. Core and slice ½ head of green cabbage into 2.5cm (1in) slices and place on the baking sheet in a single layer. Sprinkle with salt and toss in the reserved bacon fat. The leaves will separate. Return the baking sheet to the oven and roast, tossing once or twice, until browned and crisp in bits, 30–35 minutes.

Remove the baking sheet from the oven and add 3 tablespoons Xanadu pepper dream, tossing to combine. Return to the oven and continue to roast until the sauce caramelizes slightly, about 5 minutes. Remove from the oven and add the reserved bacon to the baking sheet. Toss to combine and transfer to a serving dish. Serve immediately. **Serves 4**

● Heat 2 tablespoons rapeseed oil in a large frying pan. Add **cubed aubergine (eggplant)** and cook until lightly golden. Add some sauce and toss to combine. Stir in a couple of handfuls of torn basil leaves. Serve with rice.

● For a party, serve a platter of small **savoury scones** or **biscuits**, sliced ham and this sauce for spreading.

THE BLACK VINEGAR SOLUTION

If you're like me, the type of person who loves Chinese and Southeast Asian cuisine, it's good to have an all-purpose dipping sauce recipe at your fingertips in case you suddenly need one. For example, if your local takeaway restaurant forgets to slip a container in the bag with the rest of your dinner, this sauce comes together quickly and becomes a solution in more ways than one. This recipe owes its added depth to black vinegar. Originally hailing from China, black vinegar gets its distinctive flavour from the grains with which it is made – usually a combination of rice, millet, barley and sorghum that is then fermented. You can find it in the interntational aisle at your local grocery store or Southeast Asian store. I like to plunge everything from spring rolls, fried tofu and, of course, dumplings into the inky depths of this solution.

Makes about 175ml (6fl oz)

1 teaspoon raw sesame seeds
60ml (4 tablespoons) low-sodium soy sauce
60ml (4 tablespoons) black vinegar
½ teaspoon hot chilli oil or
¼ teaspoon chilli flakes
2 teaspoons grated fresh ginger
2 teaspoons toasted sesame oil
2 tablespoons mirin
1 tablespoon chopped fresh chives

1. Heat the sesame seeds in a small frying pan over a medium-low heat, stirring constantly until lightly toasted, about 5 minutes. Transfer to a bowl.

2. Add the soy sauce, black vinegar, chilli oil, ginger, sesame oil and mirin and whisk to combine. Stir in the chives. Use immediately or store refrigerated in an airtight container for up to 2 days. Let sit at room temperature for about 30 minutes before using.

When purchasing prawns, (shrimp) always choose wild caught, as local as you can find it. Buy your prawns frozen unless you know exactly when and where they were caught. What's labelled as 'fresh' at the supermarket fish counters are usually brought in frozen anyway.

Prawn, Watercress and Pea Shoot Dumplings

Peel and devein 350g (12oz) raw prawns (shrimp). Place two-thirds of the prawns in a food processor. Coarsely chop the remaining one-third prawns on a board and transfer to a medium bowl.

To the prawns in the food processor, add 1 peeled garlic clove, 2 spring onions (white and light green parts only), 2 teaspoons chopped fresh ginger, 15g (½oz) watercress, 15g (½oz) pea shoots, 1 teaspoon low-sodium soy sauce, 2 teaspoons toasted sesame oil, 1 teaspoon sugar and 1 large egg. Pulse about 20 times until finely chopped. Transfer to the medium bowl with the prawns in it and stir in 2 tablespoons chopped spring onion greens.

Ready a small bowl of water and a package of 32 dumpling wrappers. On a clean work surface, spoon about 2 teaspoons filling into the centre of each wrapper. Use your finger to dab some water around the rim of the wrapper, then fold the wrapper in half

and, pressing hard, crease and crimp to form a tight seam. Place on a parchment-lined baking sheet sprinkled with a bit of cornflour. Repeat with the remaining filling and wrappers to create 32 dumplings. (You can freeze the dumplings on a baking sheet, then transfer to a sealable bag. They will keep for up to 2 months. No need to thaw before cooking as follows.)

Heat 2 tablespoons rapeseed oil in a large cast-iron or nonstick frying pan over a medium-high heat. Working in batches, add 11 dumplings to the pan and let cook undisturbed until the bottoms are golden brown and crisp, about 3 minutes. Add 2 tablespoons water to the pan and immediately cover with a lid. Continue to cook until all the water has evaporated and the dumplings are cooked through, about 2 minutes. Transfer to a platter and serve with the black vinegar solution.

Makes 32 dumplings

Extra Credit

● Better than takeaway: stir-fry some **leftover rice** with a scrambled egg and peas, then stir in some sauce.

● Add 50ml (2fl oz) rapeseed oil to the black vinegar solution and shake it up to form a dressing. Try it on a Chinese-inspired salad of **celery sticks** sliced on the diagonal topped with toasted cashews.

● Sauté some chicken and vegetables (**mangetout and asparagus** are good choices), then stir in the sauce at the end for a quick stir-fry.

● Boil some rice vermicelli noodles, heat them up in a pot of chicken stock and stir in this sauce to taste. Top with coriander (cilantro), grated carrots, chopped pak choi and sliced chicken breast for a killer **chicken soup**.

MAPLE BOURBON GLAZE

Here in Maine, where I've settled with my family, maple syrup is such a beloved part of the culture. There's actually a Maine Maple Sunday in March in celebration of this natural sweetener. Pure maple syrup is a labour of love that involves collecting the sap in buckets and boiling it down over wood fires. About 150 litres (40 gallons) of sap are needed to produce 3.5 litres (1 gallon) of syrup; hence the steep price tag. I always stash a bottle or two in the refrigerator to use on breakfast-related items, but I keep it in mind for savoury dishes as well since the sweetness can round out spicy, salty and rich foods. This glaze pairs maple with the smoky flavour of bourbon. It's great brushed on grilled salmon, prawns (shrimp) or chicken wings.

Makes about 750ml (1⅓ pints)

2 tablespoons extra virgin olive oil
90g (3¼oz) peeled and chopped shallots
375ml (13fl oz) bourbon whisky
185g (6½oz) pure maple syrup
60g (2¼oz) Dijon mustard
60g (2¼oz) tomato purée
120g (4¼oz) ketchup
2 teaspoons smoked paprika
½ teaspoon cayenne pepper
2 teaspoons apple cider vinegar
Sea salt and freshly ground black pepper

1. Heat the oil in a medium saucepan over a medium heat. Add the shallots and cook, stirring occasionally, until soft, about 5 minutes.

2. Off the heat, pour in the bourbon. Raise the heat to medium-high, bring to the boil and cook until the bourbon is reduced by half, 8–10 minutes.

3. Add the maple syrup, mustard, tomato purée, ketchup, smoked paprika, cayenne pepper and 120ml (4fl oz) water, stir to combine, and bring to a simmer. Cook, stirring occasionally, until the flavours develop and the mixture thickens slightly, 10–12 minutes. Stir in the vinegar and season to taste with salt and pepper.

When cooking with spirits, wine or beer, the goal is to extract the essence of flavour without the bite of booze. This means boiling off the alcohol, which evaporates at 78°C (172°F).

Extra Credit

- Brush the glaze on **bacon** slices, then bake until crisp; eat them like candy.

- Mix a one-to-one ratio of the sauce with water and pour enough over a pork shoulder or butt to halfway up the sides of a slow cooker. Cook for 8 hours, until very tender. Shred the meat to make **pulled pork sandwiches** for a crowd.

- Stir some sauce to taste into **mashed sweet potatoes** for a Thanksgiving-worthy side dish.

- Make **hash brown potatoes**, stir in leftover roast beef and drizzle with the maple bourbon glaze.

Twice-Cooked Dry-Rubbed Ribs

Preheat the oven to 150°C (300°F), Gas Mark 2. Line a baking sheet with foil and top with a piece of baking parchment. Lay a 1.3kg (3lb) slab of baby back pork ribs meat-side up on top of the paper and set aside. In a small bowl, stir together 2 teaspoons regular paprika, 2 teaspoons smoked paprika, 2 teaspoons chilli powder, 2 teaspoons garlic powder, 2 teaspoons onion powder, 2 tablespoons dark brown sugar, 2 teaspoons coarse sea salt and 1 teaspoon black pepper. Rub the spice mixture all over the ribs. Cover the baking sheet tightly with another sheet of foil and cook for about 1 hour.

Remove from the oven and spoon 200ml (7fl oz) maple bourbon glaze over the ribs. Cover and seal with foil again and return to the oven. Cook until very tender, another 1½–2 hours.

Preheat a grill or grill pan. Grill the ribs until crispy in parts, turning occasionally, 6–12 minutes total. Brush with more maple bourbon glaze, slice between the bones and serve. **Serves 4**

WAIKIKI TERIYAKI

Teriyaki sauce is due for a reappraisal. Over the years commercial versions have turned it into a sickly sweet concoction. If you make it at home though, you can control how much sugar goes in the mix. This version exploits Hawaiian cuisine's unique blend of Polynesian and Southeast Asian-influenced flavours. Putting fresh pineapple in the mix, this riff on Hawaiian barbecue sauce makes a great marinade for meats or an accompaniment for vegetables. Try it with asparagus, sweet potatoes or taro.

Makes about 440ml (15½fl oz)

215g (7½oz) chopped fresh pineapple
1 tablespoon rapeseed oil
1 tablespoon chopped fresh ginger
2 garlic cloves, finely chopped
2 tablespoons dry sherry
120ml (4fl oz) low-sodium soy sauce
70g (2½oz) dark brown sugar

1. Place the pineapple in a food processor and purée until smooth, about 2 minutes.

2. Heat the rapeseed oil in a medium saucepan over a medium heat. Add the ginger and garlic and cook until fragrant, about 1 minute. Add the sherry and cook until reduced by half, about 2 minutes. Add the puréed pineapple, soy sauce and brown sugar and cook, stirring occasionally, until heated through, about 5 minutes. Use warm, room temperature or cold. Store refrigerated in an airtight container for up to 1 week.

Extra Credit

● Use Waikiki teriyaki in place of duck sauce to dip egg rolls, **fried wontons** or vegetable tempura.

● Brush and baste oven-roasted **chicken wings** with this sauce for a sweet and tangy chicken starter.

● Cut ripe **plantains** into chunks and sauté until tender, then toss them in the pan with some of the sauce until glazed.

● Baste **pork tenderloin** with this sauce while grilling it. Slice it against the grain and spoon more sauce over the top. Serve with rice and sautéed mangetout.

Pork and Prawn Pineapple Fried Rice

Heat 2 tablespoons rapeseed oil in a large high-sided frying pan over a medium heat. Beat 2 large eggs, pour them into the pan and swirl to spread them out. Cook without stirring until just set, about 2 minutes. Use a spatula to scrape the eggs out onto a board and slice into ribbons. Set aside.

Return the pan to the hob. Season 350g (12oz) boneless pork shoulder, trimmed and cut into 1cm (½in) pieces, with 1½ teaspoons salt and ½ teaspoon black pepper. Increase the heat to medium-high. Add 1 tablespoon rapeseed oil, swirl to coat the pan, then add the pork. Cook without stirring for about 2 minutes, then continue to cook, stirring once or twice, until just cooked through, about 3 minutes more.

Add 20g (¾oz) chopped spring onions (white and light green parts), 2 tablespoons finely chopped ginger and 3 chopped garlic cloves and cook until fragrant, about 1 minute. Add 110g (4oz) chopped red pepper, 140g (5oz) chopped pineapple and 225g (8oz) peeled and deveined medium prawns (shrimp). Cook, stirring occasionally, until the prawns are opaque and curled, 3–4 minutes.

Add 400g (14oz) leftover cooked rice and toss to combine. Heat through, about 4 minutes. Stir in 100g (3½oz) baby spinach, 35g (1¼oz) chopped spring onion greens and 120ml (4fl oz) Waikiki teriyaki sauce. Toss and cook until the spinach wilts, about 2 minutes. Add the eggs and gently toss. Serve immediately, garnished with chopped toasted salted cashews and lime wedges. Drizzle with additional Waikiki teriyaki sauce. **Serves 4**

GINGER CARROT FIXER

You know that salad dressing that seems mandatory in every Japanese steakhouse in America? The one with the supernatural orange colour and addictive flavour you can't place? I've always loved it to the point of licking the bowl at the end of the meal (at least that's better than licking the chopsticks). This is my back-engineered version for the home. There are no oranges; the bright glow comes from raw carrots. The sesame oil is also key. It has a savouriness that makes you want to keep eating. This one is easy to whip up and keep around for drizzling on just about any salad. I call this one 'the fixer' because it can take the blandest ingredient to delicious in just one swipe.

Makes about 375ml (13fl oz)

3 medium carrots, peeled and cut into 2.5cm (1in) chunks
2 tablespoons finely chopped fresh ginger
2 spring onions, chopped, whites and light green parts only (save the dark greens for another use)
60ml (4 tablespoons) rice vinegar
3 tablespoons mirin
2 tablespoons low-sodium soy sauce
2 teaspoons toasted sesame oil
100ml (3½fl oz) rapeseed or grapeseed oil
Sea salt

Place the carrots, ginger, spring onions, vinegar, mirin, soy sauce, sesame oil and rapeseed oil in a high-speed blender or food processor. Blend until smooth. Season to taste with salt and blend to incorporate. Store refrigerated in an airtight container for up to 1 week.

Extra Credit

● Beyond salad, try this on cooked greens like **spinach or kale** – either sautéed as a warm side dish, or in the style of Japanese ohitashi starters (blanched, squeezed dry and doused with the sauce).

● Add some veggies to your meat **dumplings** by using this as the dipping sauce. Or use as a dunker for chicken kebabs.

Radish and Turnip Salad with Crispy Shiitakes

Divide 265g (9½oz) mesclun salad greens among four bowls. Use a mandoline or a sharp knife to thinly slice 4 radishes, 4 baby turnips or 1 medium peeled turnip and ¼ seedless cucumber. Scatter these vegetables on top of the greens.

Peel, pit and thinly slice 1 avocado and divide the slices among the four bowls. Top each bowl with a small handful of pea shoots.

Remove the stems from 175g (6oz) shiitake mushrooms and thinly slice the caps. Heat 2 tablespoons rapeseed oil in a large frying pan over a medium-high heat. When hot, add half of the mushrooms to the pan and let cook, undisturbed, until golden brown around the edges. Flip and continue to cook the mushrooms until crisp and brown, 4–6 minutes total. Transfer to a plate and sprinkle the mushrooms with salt to taste. Repeat with the remaining batch.

Top the salad bowls with the mushrooms and drizzle with ginger carrot fixer to taste. Serve immediately. **Serves 4**

● Combine equal parts of this sauce with the mother tahini (page 88), for a killer **grain-bowl topping**.

● Place small cubes of tofu on **cucumber rounds**, drizzle with the sauce, sprinkle with finely sliced spring onions and you have a party-worthy starter that's especially refreshing in the warmer months.

Herby

The Mother Pesto . . . 50

Garlic, Lemon and Mint Chimichurri . . . 52
[Grilled Sirloin, Potato and Asparagus Salad]

Salsa Verde for the Anchovy-Wary . . . 56
[Scallop Crudo with Citrus and Chillies]

The Great Shallot and Parsley Caper . . . 58
[Aubergine Crisps]

Roasted Red Pepper and Oregano Picante . . . 60
[Hot and Cold Flatbread]

Purple Basil and Almond Smash . . . 62
[Blueberry Caprese Open-Faced Sandwiches]

Thyme Grapefruit Beurre Blanc . . . 64
[Grilled Prawns with Fennel and Avocado Salad]

Herbed Brown Butter . . . 66
[Hippie Popcorn]

The Mother Pesto

Most people associate pesto with the ubiquitous combination of basil and pine nuts – a surefire winner, yes – but it's just one of many possible combos. The truth is, if you have 1) a herb or veggie base, 2) a nut or seed, 3) some sort of hard cheese, 4) garlic or something in the allium family, 5) a touch of acid and 6) lots of olive oil, you are in business, pesto-wise. A few caveats: always make sure to wash and dry your greens thoroughly. Season appropriately at the end and don't overly blend or crush. Toss a pesto with any pasta or use as a substitute for marinara on a pizza, slather it on an omelette, use as a sandwich spread . . . I could go on all day. In fact, pesto is just as good for breakfast as it is for dinner.

Makes about 250ml (9fl oz)

45g (1½oz) raw pine nuts
40g (1½oz) fresh basil leaves, thoroughly washed, dried and torn
2 garlic cloves, crushed
1 teaspoon fresh lemon juice
20g (¾oz) grated Parmesan cheese
100ml (3½fl oz) extra virgin olive oil
Sea salt and freshly ground black pepper

1. Heat the pine nuts in a small frying pan over a medium heat while stirring constantly until lightly toasted, about 6 minutes. Immediately transfer them to the bowl of a food processor to cool.

2. Add the basil to the food processor along with the garlic, lemon juice and cheese. Pulse about 40 times until very finely chopped. Continue to pulse while slowly drizzling in the olive oil until all the olive oil is incorporated and the pesto is smooth but slightly chunky. Season to taste with salt and pepper. Use immediately or place a piece of plastic directly over the top of the pesto so that it doesn't oxidize. Refrigerate in an airtight container for up to 3 days.

50

Mix It Up

Customize the mother sauce to your taste,
and to use in different ways.

Carrot-Top, Kale & Lemon Pesto

Replace the basil with 50g (1¾oz) carrot-top leaves removed from the stems of carrots and 50g (1¾oz) chopped kale leaves. Add 1 tablespoon lemon zest and increase the lemon juice to 2 tablespoons.

Rocket, Walnut & Pecorino Pesto

Replace the basil with baby rocket (arugula), replace the pine nuts with raw walnuts and replace the Parmesan with 40g (1½oz) grated pecorino cheese.

Parsley, Sun-Dried Tomato & Cashew Pesto

Replace the basil with 40g (1½oz) chopped fresh flat-leaf parsley, add 55g (2oz) chopped sun-dried tomatoes and replace the pine nuts with raw cashews.

Coriander, Pumpkin Seed & Manchego Pesto

Replace the basil with 60g (2¼oz) chopped fresh coriander (cilantro), replace the pine nuts with 70g (2½oz) raw shelled pumpkin seeds (pepita) and replace the Parmesan cheese with grated mild Manchego cheese.

Extra Credit

• Thin out any of the pestos with some water and a bit of vinegar to make a divine **salad dressing**.

• Do as they do in Provence and stir pesto into a **veggie soup** (but then in this case call it pistou).

• Turn your **potato salad** super-green: Ditch the mayo, add blanched green beans and toss everything with pesto to coat.

• Top a piece of toasted **rustic bread** with fresh mozzarella, chopped fresh tomatoes and a spoonful of any one of the pestos. Easy Caprese!

GARLIC, LEMON AND MINT CHIMICHURRI

An Argentinean *parilla* without chimichurri would be like a French fry stand without ketchup. This classic steak sauce, usually consisting of some variety of fresh herbs, aromatics and oil, is delicious spooned over any type of grilled meat or seafood. My take on chimichurri incorporates notes of mint and lots of citrus, which lightens things up, making for a sauce versatile enough to pair with veggies, too.

Makes about 375ml (13fl oz)

100g (3½oz) fresh flat-leaf parsley stems and leaves
15g (½oz) fresh mint leaves
2 tablespoons fresh lemon zest
2 garlic cloves, chopped
2 teaspoons brown sugar
3 tablespoons fresh lemon juice
150ml (5fl oz) extra virgin olive oil
Sea salt
Pinch of chilli flakes (optional)

1. Combine the parsley, mint, lemon zest, garlic and brown sugar in a food processor. Pulse a few times, until the herbs are coarsely chopped. With the processor running, add the lemon juice, then slowly drizzle in the olive oil in a thin stream until combined. Season to taste with salt and the chilli flakes, if desired.

2. Use immediately or store refrigerated in an airtight container for up to 3 days.

In Argentina, *parillas*, wood-fired meat-centric restaurants, are ubiquitous. Each *parilla* has its own version of chimichurri. Legend has it chimichurri was named in honour of an Irishman called Jimmy McCurry who supported Argentina's independence in the 19th century. The locals had trouble pronouncing his name; hence *chimichurri*.

Extra Credit

- Roast a bunch of **carrot chunks** then toss them with this sauce – delicious warm or at room temperature.

- Stir into brown rice along with some fresh peas, baby spinach and crumbled feta for a **whole-meal salad** to bring to work.

- For a summery veggie dinner, grill a lot of asparagus and some **aubergine (eggplant)**. Roughly chop the two, then add to pasta and toss with the chimichurri sauce.

- Steam **clams** with a little water in a covered pot until they open, stir in this sauce and serve over fregola or couscous.

Grilled Sirloin, Potato and Asparagus Salad

Put 450g (1lb) small new potatoes in a medium saucepan and add enough cold water to cover by 5cm (2in). Bring to the boil and cook over a high heat until the potatoes are tender, about 10 minutes. Drain the potatoes and cut each in half. Transfer to a large bowl with 1 bunch trimmed asparagus spears. Drizzle the potatoes and asparagus lightly with olive oil and season to taste with salt and pepper.

Preheat a grill or grill pan to a medium-high heat. Add the potatoes and asparagus to the grill and cook, turning occasionally, until grill marks form and the asparagus is crisp tender. Transfer the potatoes and asparagus to four large plates or bowls. Top each with 15g (½oz) baby rocket (arugula).

Season two 225g (8oz) sirloin steaks liberally with salt and pepper. Lightly oil the grill or grill pan and grill the steak for 4–6 minutes per side for medium (60–63°C/140–145°F) or 3–5 minutes per side for medium rare (54–57°C/130–135°F). Transfer the steak to a board and let rest for about 5 minutes. Slice the steaks across the grain and add to the plates with the vegetables. Drizzle with chimichurri sauce. Serve warm or room temperature. **Serves 4**

SALSA VERDE FOR THE ANCHOVY-WARY

Not to be mistaken with the tomatillo-laden Mexican sauce of the same name, this classic fresh green sauce blends fresh herbs, tart citrus and briny capers. If you can be bothered, I recommend using the authentic hand-chopping technique to preserve and heighten the delicate flavours of the herbs – but if you don't have time I won't judge you. This sauce adds life to anything from veggies (try with artichokes) and bread (especially focaccia) to seafood and steak.

While the classic version calls for anchovies, which I love, I've left them out in deference to those of you who do not. You'll still get a healthy dose of umami flavour from the capers here. But if you are anchovy friendly, try chopping up a few fillets to stir in, or use a teaspoon of anchovy paste.

Makes about 190g (6½oz)

2 garlic cloves
1 teaspoon sea salt
1 teaspoon orange zest
1 teaspoon lemon zest
2 tablespoons fresh lemon juice
100ml (3½fl oz) extra virgin olive oil
15g (½oz) chopped fresh flat-leaf parsley
10g (¼oz) chopped fresh basil
3 tablespoons chopped fresh mint
1 tablespoon drained capers
Freshly ground black pepper

1. Place the garlic cloves on a board. Using the side of a chef's knife, press to crush the garlic. Add the salt to the garlic and continue to chop and press with the side of the knife until a paste forms.

2. Transfer the salted garlic to a bowl along with the orange zest, lemon zest, lemon juice and olive oil. Stir in the parsley, basil, mint and capers. Season to taste with pepper. Store refrigerated for up to 2 days. Bring back to room temperature before using.

Extra Credit

- Stir into a pot of **white beans** and serve with rustic bread for a divine meatless supper.

- Thread prawns (shrimp) and **courgette (zucchini) chunks** onto skewers, brush with olive oil and grill. Then paint with this sauce and serve more for dipping.

- Marinate **bocconcini** (small mozzarella balls) in this sauce for up to a day, then serve with toothpicks for a party. Yum!

- Warm a few tablespoons of olive oil over a low heat. Add 200g (7oz) good-quality **olives** and heat through. Pour the sauce over the top and serve as a warm marinated olive starter.

Scallop Crudo with Citrus and Chillies

Remove the side muscles if any are still attached from 225g (8oz) day boat or sushi-grade dry sea scallops. Slice each scallop horizontally in half and place on a large platter.

Use a sharp knife to carefully cut the top and bottom peel off of 4 oranges and 1 lime. Slice the remaining peel and pith away from the flesh and discard. Cut between the membranes to segment the oranges and lime, working over a medium bowl to catch the segments and any juices. Spoon the citrus segments and juices over the scallops.

Thinly slice 1 Anaheim or red jalapeño chilli and sprinkle over the scallops. Generously drizzle the scallops with some of the salsa verde. Season to taste with salt and pepper. Serve immediately. **Serves 4**

Briny capers, the signature ingredient of salsa verde, may look like tiny olives at first, but they are in fact the pickled flower buds that come from a shrub that grows wild in the Mediterranean.

THE GREAT SHALLOT AND PARSLEY CAPER

This wine and herb sauce is simple and classic, and it adds a pop of flavour to savoury dishes of every stripe. Loosely inspired by the flavours of maître d'hôtel, the compound butter frequently used in French cuisine, this sauce uses as its foundation shallots, parsley and capers, plus some fresh lemon juice to brighten things up. It doesn't take long to cook and will be a welcome addition poured over vegetables like asparagus and squash, a delicate piece of fish, or even a pan-seared steak like the ones found at a French brasserie. *Vive le roi!*

Makes about 120ml (4fl oz)

1 tablespoon unsalted butter, plus 2 tablespoons cold unsalted butter, cut into small pieces
1 tablespoon extra virgin olive oil
1 medium shallot, chopped
60ml (4 tablespoons) dry white wine
60ml (4 tablespoons) low-sodium chicken or vegetable stock
2 tablespoons drained capers
1 teaspoon lemon zest
1 tablespoon fresh lemon juice
3 tablespoons chopped fresh flat-leaf parsley
Sea salt and freshly ground black pepper

1. Melt 1 tablespoon of the butter with the olive oil in a medium frying pan over a medium heat. Add the shallot and cook until softened, about 3 minutes.

2. Add the wine and cook until reduced by half, about 3 minutes. Add the stock and capers and cook until reduced by half, about 3 minutes. Turn off the heat, stir in the lemon zest and juice, then whisk in the 2 tablespoons cold butter, a little at a time, until the sauce thickens. Stir in the fresh chopped parsley. Season lightly with salt and pepper. Serve immediately.

Extra Credit

- Drizzle on top of roasted broccoli, **Brussels sprouts** or cauliflower for a flavourful side dish.

- Toss the sauce with pasta, along with fresh olives, rocket (arugula) and shredded **rotisserie chicken** for an easy dinner.

- Make **Caprese towers**: stack layers of sliced beefsteak tomatoes and sliced mozzarella. Warm in a 180°C (350°F), Gas Mark 4 oven until the cheese begins to melt. Then drizzle with the sauce and sprinkle torn basil leaves on top.

- Cook skin-on **chicken breasts** in a pan until crispy and cooked through, then nap with this sauce on the plate. Serve with boiled potatoes for a bistro-worthy supper.

Aubergine Crisps

Slice 2 Italian aubergines (eggplant) (about 600g/1lb 5oz total) crossways into 5mm (¼in) slices. Place in a large bowl with 35g (1¼oz) cornflour and toss to combine and thoroughly coat.

Pour 2.5cm (1in) of rapeseed oil (about 900ml/1½ pints) into a large pot and heat over a medium-high heat until it reaches 182°C (360°F) on a deep-fry thermometer. Working in batches, fry the aubergine for 3–4 minutes total, flipping halfway through cooking, until golden brown and crisp on both sides. If the oil starts to smoke, lower the heat. Drain off extra fat by transferring the aubergine with a slotted spoon or spider to a kitchen paper-lined plate. Lightly sprinkle with salt. Repeat with the remaining aubergine slices.

Transfer to a serving platter. Drizzle with the wine and herb sauce and a squeeze of fresh lemon. Serve immediately. **Serves 4**

ROASTED RED PEPPER AND OREGANO PICANTE

One reliable indicator of a good restaurant is the bread. In Brooklyn my husband and I frequented this little Italian place that brought to the table hot, chewy bread with a ramekin of what looked like tomato sauce, except it wasn't. Half good olive oil and half smashed, thickened tomatoes with hits of herbs and garlic, it was saltier and more intense than pasta sauce; we'd invariably ask for more. This is an homage with a twist: I've swapped roasted red peppers for most of the tomatoes and fresh oregano for the herb mix. Besides being a killer dipper for bread, it also works well as a condiment for meat or chicken.

Makes about 440ml (15½fl oz)

2 medium red peppers
45ml (3 tablespoons) extra virgin olive oil
4 garlic cloves, thinly sliced
¼–¾ teaspoon chilli flakes
1 tablespoon tomato purée
55g (2oz) canned crushed or finely chopped tomatoes
1 tablespoon chopped fresh oregano
1 teaspoon sugar
Sea salt and freshly ground black pepper

1. Place the peppers on a baking sheet and grill them, turning occasionally until completely charred, about 15 minutes. Transfer to a medium bowl, cover with clingfilm (plastic wrap) and let steam for about 10 minutes. Carefully peel and deseed the peppers and finely chop them.

2. Heat the olive oil and garlic in a medium saucepan over a medium-low heat. Cook, stirring occasionally, until the garlic is very soft and just beginning to turn golden, about 5 minutes. Add the chilli flakes and tomato purée and stir to combine.

3. Stir in the roasted red pepper, tomatoes, oregano, 60ml (4 tablespoons) water and the sugar. Raise the heat to medium, bring just to a simmer and cook, stirring occasionally until the flavours develop, about 3 minutes. Season to taste with salt and pepper.

Extra Credit

● Swap out for tomato sauce to make a **lasagne** picante.

● Warm up some corn tortillas, spread with refried beans, cheese, shredded lettuce, corn and chopped fresh tomatoes, then top with this sauce for perfect **veggie tacos**.

Hot and Cold Flatbread

Stir 2¼ teaspoons (1 packet) active dry yeast and 1 tablespoon sugar into 375ml (13fl oz) slightly warm (43°C/110°F) water. Let stand for 5 minutes. In a large bowl, whisk together 400g (14oz) plain flour and 2 teaspoons sea salt. Add the yeast water and 3 tablespoons olive oil and mix until a soft dough comes together. Turn the dough out onto a lightly floured work surface. Knead, adding more flour if necessary, until the dough becomes more elastic, about 3 minutes. Form the dough into a ball, transfer it to a lightly oiled large bowl and cover loosely with a piece of clingfilm. (plastic wrap) Let rise until doubled in size, 1–1½ hours.

Punch down the dough and turn it out onto a lightly floured surface. Divide the dough into 4 equal balls. Use your hands to gently stretch each piece of dough into 20cm (8in) diameter round.

Preheat a grill pan over a medium-high heat. Brush with olive oil and add one flatbread to the pan. Cook for 8–10 minutes total, flipping halfway through cooking. Repeat with the remaining dough.

Spread 90ml (6 tablespoons) picante sauce on top of each flatbread, then top each with 85g (3oz) sliced mozzarella and a generous handful of rocket (arugula). Drizzle with olive oil and season. **Serves 4**

● Sauté sliced onion in olive oil in a cast-iron frying pan. Stir in the sauce, then crack 6–8 **eggs** over the top. Bake at 200°C (400°F), Gas Mark 6 until the egg whites are set.

● Place rounds of **goat's cheese** on crackers, then dollop with this sauce. Pair with a robust red wine.

PURPLE BASIL AND ALMOND SMASH

Purple basil: I'll see it at the farmers' market, make a mental note to buy a bunch next time, then miss my chance. Its growing season is relatively short. Well, last year I finally planted some and it grew like wildfire, causing my issue to go from can't get any to what do I do with it? Fortunately a saucy idea came to mind. This recipe is the result: it's great on a slew of dishes, thanks to purple basil's slightly clove-like, subtly spicy flavour and striking colour. It is reminiscent of pesto, but since it has no cheese, it will still please your vegan friends. And if you miss the short seasonal window, green basil can always be substituted.

Makes about 185g (6½oz)

2 tablespoons raw almonds
½ teaspoon sea salt
20g (¾oz) purple or green basil leaves
1 tablespoon lemon zest
1 tablespoon fresh lemon juice
1–2 teaspoons thinly sliced fresh chilli, such as red jalapeño
100ml (3½fl oz) extra virgin olive oil

In the bowl of a food processor, combine the almonds and salt and process until finely ground. Add the basil, lemon zest, lemon juice and chilli and pulse until finely minced. Slowly drizzle in the olive oil while pulsing to combine. Serve immediately.

Extra Credit

- Toss cold shredded **chicken breast** with capers and cooked and cooled new potatoes, then drizzle with the sauce for a great picnic salad.

- Roll **roasted corn on the cob** through this sauce for extra crunch and colour. Yum!

- Dip raw **peppers** and/or fennel into this sauce.

- Sprinkle sliced **peaches or nectarines** in coupe glasses with this sauce (omit the chilli, if you prefer) for an elegant palate cleanser or a light summer dessert.

Blueberry Caprese Open-Faced Sandwiches

Preheat the oven to 190°C (375°F), Gas Mark 5. Place 4 slices of dark rye bread on a baking sheet and drizzle each with 2 teaspoons olive oil. Toast in the oven until just beginning to crisp, 6–8 minutes. Divide the bread among four plates.

Layer each slice of toast with 2 slices prosciutto, 55g (2oz) burrata or buffalo mozzarella cheese, 15g (½oz) rocket (arugula), 2 tablespoons microgreens, some basil leaves and 30g (1oz) halved blueberries. Drizzle with the purple basil and almond smash. Serve immediately.

Serves 4

Thai basil and lemon basil are just the tip of the iceherb – sorry, iceberg. Check farmers' markets or seed catalogues to grow your own; there are more than forty varieties from which to choose.

THYME GRAPEFRUIT BEURRE BLANC

I like to think of myself as a super smeller or, more elegantly put, an olfactory wizard. For better or worse, I can't help noticing smells, of any kind, and commenting on them – a habit, I've come to realize, which may annoy the less nasally inclined. In any event, this sauce is good for those like me who are keen to scents. It is equally pleasing to the nose and the taste buds. Slightly sweet, tart and herby, this feels like summer in a pot. It is a great addition to foods that are light or bland, such as steamed vegetables or chicken breast. The aromatherapy qualities are an added benefit.

Makes about 175g (6oz)

1 tablespoon ruby red or yellow grapefruit zest
300ml (10fl oz) fresh ruby red or yellow grapefruit juice (from 2–3 grapefruits)
3 tablespoons honey
1 sprig thyme, plus 1 teaspoon chopped fresh thyme leaves
2 teaspoons extra virgin olive oil
3 tablespoons cold unsalted butter, cut into small pieces
Sea salt and freshly ground black pepper

1. In a medium saucepan, combine the grapefruit zest, grapefruit juice, honey, thyme sprig and olive oil. Bring to the boil over a high heat and cook until reduced by half, 6–8 minutes.

2. Turn off the heat and stir in the chopped thyme, then whisk in the butter, a little at a time, until thickened. Season to taste with salt and pepper. Remove the thyme sprig and blend with a stick blender or whisk until frothy. Serve warm or at room temperature.

Extra Credit

• Drizzle over pan-seared scallops, salmon, **mild white fish** or even lobster.

• Spoon over steamed **green beans**, then top with crunchy toasted almonds and breadcrumbs for a winning side dish.

• Use thyme and grapefruit beurre blanc as a dipper for **coconut-crusted prawns (shrimp)** or chicken breast.

• Roast leeks or **spring onions** until charred in spots (as they do in Catalonia), then drizzle this sauce on top.

Grilled Prawns with Fennel and Avocado Salad

Place 225g (8oz) peeled and deveined large prawns (shrimp) in a medium bowl with 1 teaspoon salt, ½ teaspoon black pepper and 1 tablespoon olive oil. Toss to combine.

Meanwhile, use a sharp knife to carefully cut the top and bottom peel off 2 ruby red grapefruits. Slice the remaining peel and pith away from the flesh and discard. Cut between the membranes to segment the grapefruits over a medium bowl to catch the segments and any juices.

Trim the bottom and cut the fronds off 1 large bulb of fennel. Reserve 25g (1oz) fronds. Thinly slice the fennel and add to the bowl with the grapefruit. Halve, pit and chop 1 avocado and add to the bowl. Season to taste with salt and pepper and toss to combine.

Divide the salad among four plates. Preheat a grill or grill pan to medium heat and grill the prawns for 2–3 minutes per side, or until cooked through and curled. Top each salad with some prawns. Drizzle each plate with the grapefruit beurre blanc. Serve immediately. **Serves 4**

HERBED BROWN BUTTER

Browned butter seems to be popping up all over the place these days at restaurants and in people's kitchens, but if you're like me, or pretty much anybody else, you never tire of it. The magic happens when you cook butter past the stage of just melted, until the milk solids float up to the top and begin to caramelize, at which point the butter turns from golden yellow to golden brown. The aroma at this stage will go from creamy to nutty, as will the flavour. By itself, brown butter can be added to just about anything from meat, fish and vegetables to desserts. Here I've added fresh herbs to balance out the richness with a hit of fresh green flavour.

Makes about 60ml (4 tablespoons)

4 tablespoons unsalted butter
1 teaspoon finely chopped fresh flat-leaf parsley
1 teaspoon finely chopped fresh sage
1 teaspoon finely chopped fresh thyme leaves
½ teaspoon finely chopped fresh rosemary leaves
Sea salt and freshly ground black pepper

In a small saucepan, heat the butter over a medium heat until it has melted, about 4 minutes. Continue to cook without stirring until the butter has a nutty aroma and the milk solids begin to turn golden brown around the edges, another 3–4 minutes. Turn off the heat and immediately stir in the herbs and season to taste with salt and pepper. Serve right away.

Extra Credit

● Stir herbed brown butter into **rice or couscous** with some chopped toasted almonds for a divine pilaf.

● Give **turkey leftovers** a second chance by drizzling them with this sauce.

● Make **savoury crêpes** (or Italian-style crespelle), roll them around a filling of a soft cheese like ricotta, then drape them with this sauce for a decadent brunch offering.

● Toss with **ravioli** or gnocchi, ideally those made with butternut squash.

Hippie Popcorn

Place 45ml (3 tablespoons) rapeseed oil and 50g (1¾oz) popcorn kernels in a very large pot and cover with a lid. Have oven gloves or tea towels ready. Heat over a medium-high heat until you start to hear popping sounds, about 4 minutes.

Using oven gloves, shake continuously over the heat. Continue to shake as the popping increases in speed. When it starts to slow down to a crawl (2–3 seconds between

pops), after about 3 minutes, take the pot off the heat and continue to shake until you no longer hear popping.

Immediately pour the popcorn into a large bowl. Drizzle with the herbed brown butter, sprinkle with 2 teaspoons nutritional yeast and season to taste with salt. Toss well and serve immediately. **Makes about 75g (2½oz)**

Fruity

The Mother Pomodoro . . . 70

Cherry Sherry Glaze . . . 72
[Sliced Duck Breast with Duck Fat Croutons]

Plum, Tangerine and Five-Spice Jiang . . . 74
[Pan-Fried Pork Chops with Spring Onions]

Grape, Corainder, Chilli and Lime Nam Chim . . . 76
[Rice Bowl with Marinated Grilled Chicken]

Pomegranate-Lemon Reduction . . . 78
[Fried Cauliflower with Pomegranate, Parsley and Yogurt]

Cranapple Double-Ginger Relish . . . 80
[Homemade Granola and Yogurt Parfaits]

Fig and Balsamic Agrodolce . . . 82
[Pan-Roasted Pork Tenderloin with Rosemary]

Downright Upright Apple Sauce . . . 84
[Mashed Potato Pancakes with Soured Cream, Chives and Bacon]

The Mother Pomodoro

Contrary to the popular misconception, the tomato is not a vegetable but a fruit. I consider tomato sauce a pantry staple – countless recipes call for it. Having an arsenal of sauce at the ready makes cooking dinner a snap, and the variations opposite allow you to keep your meals interesting with just a few additions. I usually make a big batch and keep some in my refrigerator for the week. The rest goes into plastic freezer-safe containers or zip-tight plastic bags for up to six months. Your grandmother may have spent all day cooking her famous sauce and I'm sure it was delicious, but if you don't have all day to spare, this quick iteration is pretty darn good, at a fraction of the labour time.

Makes about 750g (1lb 10oz)

2 garlic cloves, chopped

45ml (3 tablespoons) extra virgin olive oil

800g (1lb 12oz) canned crushed or finely chopped tomatoes

2 teaspoons dried Italian seasoning

1 tablespoon sugar

Sea salt

Pinch of chilli flakes (optional)

1. Combine the garlic and olive oil in a medium saucepan over a medium-low heat. Cook, stirring occasionally, until the garlic just begins to soften and the oil is fragrant, about 4 minutes. Carefully stir in the tomatoes, dried herbs and sugar. Raise the heat to medium, stir and bring to a simmer. Continue to cook, stirring constantly, until the flavours develop and the sauce thickens slightly, about 20 minutes.

2. Stir in salt to taste. Add the chilli flakes, if desired. Use immediately or store refrigerated in an airtight container for up to 1 week or freeze for up to 6 months.

Mix It Up

Customize the mother sauce to your taste,
and to use in different ways.

Creamy Parmesan Pomodoro

Stir in 90ml (6 tablespoons) double cream, 20g (¾oz) finely grated Parmesan cheese and 10g (¼oz) chopped fresh basil over a medium-low heat until smooth and creamy.

Puttanesca Sauce

Mix in 100g (3½oz) coarsely chopped pitted Kalamata olives, 2 teaspoons anchovy paste and 1 tablespoon drained capers.

Diavolo Sauce

Add 90g (3¼oz) chopped roasted red pepper, 1 chopped fresh Fresno or red jalapeño chilli and 10g (¼oz) chopped fresh flat-leaf parsley and stir to combine.

Fresh Tomato, Herb & Garlic Sauce

Stir in 250g (9oz) chopped fresh tomatoes, 20g (¾oz) mixed chopped fresh herbs, such as oregano, parsley, rosemary, thyme and basil, and 1 finely chopped garlic clove.

Extra Credit

● Any one of the tomato sauces will be a workhorse with any shaped **pasta**, on top of pizza or as a dip for warm bread.

● Place some pomodoro in a few greased ramekins and top each with 1–2 **eggs** and a sprinkle of Parmesan. Bake at 200°C (400°F), Gas Mark 6 until the whites are opaque, 8–12 minutes.

● Roast potatoes, **broccoli**, aubergine (eggplant), fennel and green beans and serve with fresh tomato, herb and garlic sauce for a bright and flavourful vegetarian feast.

● Use any one of these sauces to make a standout chicken or **aubergine Parm.**

CHERRY SHERRY GLAZE

This recipe is inspired by Ginjinha or Ginja, a tart cherry liqueur that's famous in Portugal. Ginja varies in quality from the cheap and artificial variety to the sublime, authentic and (obviously) more expensive bottle. When I finally had some of the good stuff, I couldn't believe the flavour. Ginjinha is great to use in cooking, but since it can be difficult to locate, I used dry sherry and cherries as the base for this sauce instead. Cherry sherry glaze is a slightly sweet, tart, full-bodied sauce that is perfect for cutting through the richness of game meats, such as duck, venison or goose, or with pork tenderloin or turkey. It's also fabulous as part of a cheese plate.

Makes about 565ml (1 pint)

1 tablespoon extra virgin olive oil
1 medium shallot, finely chopped
2 garlic cloves, finely chopped
350g (12oz) pitted cherries, fresh or frozen and thawed
175ml (6fl oz) dry sherry
1 bay leaf
175ml (6fl oz) low-sodium chicken stock
2 tablespoons sugar
2 teaspoons cornflour
2 tablespoons chopped fresh tarragon
2 tablespoons cold unsalted butter
Sea salt and freshly ground black pepper

1. Heat the olive oil in a large frying pan over a medium heat. Add the shallot and garlic and cook until fragrant, about 1 minute.

2. Turn the heat off and stir in the cherries, sherry and bay leaf, then simmer over a medium-high heat until the alcohol cooks off, about 8 minutes.

3. In a small bowl, whisk together the chicken stock, sugar and cornflour. Pour the chicken stock mixture into the cherry mixture, bring to the boil and cook, stirring occasionally, until slightly thickened, 3–4 minutes. Turn the heat off and whisk in the tarragon and butter until the sauce is slightly thickened and glossy. Season to taste with salt and pepper. The sauce will keep in the refrigerator for several days.

Extra Credit

● Serve in place of cranberry sauce to accompany **turkey or chicken at Thanksgiving** or whenever.

● Sandwich some **roasted pork** between 2 pieces of multigrain or rye bread along with bitter greens, such as rocket (arugula) or dandelion, some Dijon mustard and cherry sherry glaze.

72

Sliced Duck Breast with Duck Fat Croutons

Preheat the oven to 190°C (375°F), Gas Mark 5. Ready a parchment-lined baking sheet. Place 4 duck breasts, about 175g (6oz) each, skin-side up on a board and pat dry. Using a sharp knife, make 4 or 5 parallel slits on a diagonal, cutting just through the skin. Rotate the breasts 45 degrees and score in the other direction, creating a diamond pattern. Sprinkle all over with salt and pepper.

Heat a large cast-iron or ovenproof heavy-bottomed frying pan over a medium-high heat. When the pan is hot, add the duck breasts, skin-side down, to the pan. Cook until the fat is rendered and the skin is golden brown and crisp, about 5 minutes. Use tongs to flip the duck breasts over and

sear for 4 minutes more. Transfer to the prepared baking sheet. Pour the duck fat into a small bowl and reserve the pan. Cut 150g (5½oz) rustic bread into 5cm (2in) cubes. Scatter the bread cubes around the duck breasts on the baking sheet and drizzle with 3 tablespoons of the reserved duck fat. Lightly season the bread cubes with salt. Transfer the pan to the oven and roast until the duck is cooked through, 10–12 minutes. Let the duck rest for about 5 minutes.

Transfer the duck breasts to a board and slice each across the grain. Place each breast on a plate along with some of the croutons. Drizzle with warm cherry sherry glaze and serve immediately. **Serves 4**

● Mix some of the cooled cherry sherry glaze with softened butter and use as a topping for biscuits or **scones**.

● Drizzle over **sautéed kale** or baby pak choi for a sweet and savoury combo.

PLUM, TANGERINE AND FIVE-SPICE JIANG

It's hard to find a perfectly ripe plum in the supermarket. They usually seem dry, too tart and obviously picked before their prime. That's too bad because fresh, perfectly ripe plums are incredibly juicy, sweet and fragrant with a delicate slightly floral flavour. So I have devised ways of sugaring, cooking, baking and otherwise preserving them to try to keep that flavour going as long as I can. This recipe was inspired by my need to make underripe plums taste good and also by the moo shu from our local Chinese restaurant. To me, the one element that makes moo shu worth the price of admission is the smear of rich, sweet, thick plum sauce or jiang. My version is chunky and a lot fresher tasting than the standard variety. Try it served with Chinese fare but also any rich meat, from pork and dark meat turkey to duck or goose.

Makes 750ml (1⅓ pints)

60ml (4 tablespoons) fresh tangerine juice, squeezed from 2 tangerines
1 teaspoon cornflour
1 tablespoon rapeseed oil
1 tablespoon grated fresh ginger
2 garlic cloves, thinly sliced
675g (1lb 8oz) ripe plums (about 5), halved, pitted and coarsely chopped
2 tablespoons finely chopped fresh tangerine peel
70g (2½oz) dark brown sugar
1 teaspoon five-spice powder
2 tablespoons low-sodium soy sauce
Sea salt

1. In a small bowl, whisk the tangerine juice with the cornflour until the cornflour dissolves.

2. Heat the oil over a medium heat in a large frying pan. Add the ginger and garlic and cook until fragrant, about 1 minute.

3. Add the plums, tangerine peel, brown sugar, five-spice powder and 60ml (4 tablespoons) water and stir to combine. Cook, stirring, until the plums are heated through but still hold their shape, about 8 minutes.

4. Stir in the tangerine juice mixture, bring to a simmer and cook until slightly thickened, about 3 minutes. Stir in the soy sauce and season to taste with salt. Serve immediately or store refrigerated in an airtight container for up to 3 days.

- Bathe **pulled pork** in this jiang instead of regular barbecue sauce, then make sandwiches with soft buns and shredded cabbage.

- Make an easy **lunch bowl** by tossing cooked brown rice, lettuce, chopped spring onions, coriander (cilantro) and some cooked shredded chicken with the sauce.

- Serve this sauce in place of cranberry sauce alongside dark meat chicken or **turkey** to throw some Chinese flair into Thanksgiving.

- Skip ordering takeaway and toss wide rice **noodles** and sautéed kale with the sauce instead.

Pan-Fried Pork Chops with Spring Onions

Bring four 2cm (¾in) thick, centre-cut, bone-in pork chops (about 900g/2lb total) to room temperature. Pat dry using kitchen paper and liberally season all over with salt and pepper.

Heat a large cast-iron or heavy-bottomed frying pan over a medium-high heat and, once hot, add about 1 tablespoon rapeseed oil. Add the pork chops and let cook without moving until they are golden brown on one side, 3–4 minutes. Flip and cook the remaining side until golden brown and cooked through, 3–4 minutes more. Transfer to a platter and let rest about 5 minutes.

Add 8 whole spring onions to the pan used for the pork chops. Over a medium heat, sear them slightly (about 3–4 minutes). Serve each chop with a couple of spring onions and the plum sauce on top, with rice on the side if you like. **Serves 4**

Maceration, when applied in the culinary sense, is a term most often reserved for fruit: You add liquor, vinegar and/or sugar to draw the moisture out, soften up the flesh and add flavour, creating a sauce-like syrup.

GRAPE, CORIANDER, CHILLI AND LIME NAM CHIM

I love fresh grapes, but I always find it hard to get through a whole bag. Here's a great way to use the stray leftovers before they become squishy. Sweet, savoury, tart and a little spicy all in one, this Thai-inspired fresh sauce will expand your grape repertoire, or should I say your grape-toire. It's sure to enhance anything lean and grilled. I suggest a mix of different colours of grapes here, but if you have just one variety on hand, it will still come out just as tasty.

Makes about 440ml (15½fl oz)

75g (2½oz) green seedless grapes, coarsely chopped
75g (2½oz) red seedless grapes, coarsely chopped
75g (2½oz) black seedless grapes, coarsely chopped
½ medium jalapeño, deseeded and finely chopped
1 teaspoon lime zest
1 tablespoon fresh lime juice
1 tablespoon fish sauce
25g (1oz) roughly chopped fresh coriander (cilantro)

In a medium bowl, combine the grapes, jalapeño, lime zest, lime juice, fish sauce and coriander. Stir to combine and let sit at room temperature for about 30 minutes, tossing once or twice until the flavours develop. Use immediately or store refrigerated in an airtight container for up to 2 days.

Extra Credit

● Spoon some of the sauce over cooked chicken and more coriander in a flour tortilla for a Thai-Mexican **fusion wrap**.

● Stir 100ml (3½fl oz) rapeseed oil into the sauce, then toss with shredded green and red cabbage for a tangy **slaw**.

● Toss the nam chim sauce with leftover **wild rice** and fresh torn basil for a quick side dish.

● Pulse the sauce in a food processor until finely chopped, stir in a few splashes of rice vinegar and serve with raw **oysters** on the half shell for a Thai-style mignonette.

Rice Bowl with Marinated Grilled Chicken

In a large bowl, whisk together 1 tablespoon rapeseed oil, 2 tablespoons low-sodium soy sauce, 1 tablespoon fish sauce, 2 tablespoons dark brown sugar, 2 tablespoons fresh lime juice, 2 teaspoons lime zest, 1 teaspoon grated fresh ginger, 1 teaspoon garlic powder and 1 tablespoon curry powder.

Add 2 boneless, skinless chicken breasts (550g/1lb 4oz total) sliced into 2.5cm (1in) cubes directly into the bowl and toss thoroughly to coat with the marinade. Cover and refrigerate for about 1 hour. Meanwhile, soak four 25cm (10in) wooden skewers in water for about 30 minutes before using them.

Evenly divide and thread the chicken breasts onto the skewers. Discard any leftover marinade. Preheat a grill or grill pan to a medium-high heat. Lightly oil the grill and cook the chicken pieces on all sides until grill marks form and the chicken is cooked through, about 10 minutes total.

Carefully slide the grilled chicken off the skewers into four bowls filled with cooked rice. Top each with some of the nam chim sauce and garnish with crushed roasted peanuts, a lime wedge and coriander sprigs. **Serves 4**

POMEGRANATE-LEMON REDUCTION

Pomegranate molasses is one of the quintessential Middle Eastern sauces. It adds an acidic burst that cuts right through fatty meats like beef or lamb, fried foods, creamy desserts – anything rich, really – and its deep ruby colour is beautiful to behold. I used to buy it in specialty food shops, but after moving away from Brooklyn, I've found it tricky to locate. Now I make my own. As you'll see it's easy as ABC. Just remember, it turns quickly from syrup to burnt candy, so don't get any ideas about going on a beer run while it's cooking. My version is more lemony and less sweet than the store-bought type. One of the perks of being your own saucier is the ability to tweak recipes according to your own taste.

Make about 120ml (4fl oz)

500ml (18fl oz) pomegranate juice
2 tablespoons sugar
1 teaspoon lemon zest
1 tablespoon fresh lemon juice

1. Combine the pomegranate juice, sugar and lemon zest in a medium saucepan and bring to the boil over a high heat, stirring occasionally until the sugar dissolves, about 4 minutes.

2. Continue to boil, stirring occasionally, until thickened slightly and reduced to 120ml (4fl oz), about 12 minutes. Stir in the lemon juice. Cool to room temperature and then store refrigerated in a squirt bottle or an airtight container for up to 1 month.

Extra Credit

● Mix the pomegranate-lemon reduction with sparkling water, an extra splash of fresh lemon juice, crushed fresh mint leaves and ice cubes for a nifty **spritzer**. Add vodka to up the ante.

● Drizzle the sauce over **ice cream** and top with chopped pistachios.

● Use as a dip for spiced chicken or **beef kebabs**.

● Spoon onto fruit salad to add a red flavour jolt. Or stir into vanilla, lemon or natural **yogurt** for a healthy snack.

Fried Cauliflower with Pomegranate, Parsley and Yogurt

Cut 1 head of cauliflower into 5cm (2in) florets and set aside. You should have about 450g (1lb) florets. Combine 2 large eggs, 120ml (4fl oz) room-temperature water and 1 teaspoon salt in a bowl and whisk until frothy. Add 75g (2½oz) cornflour and whisk until a smooth thin batter is formed.

Pour 2.5cm (1in) rapeseed oil (about 900ml/1½ pints) into a large pot and heat over a medium-high heat until a drop of the batter sizzles in the oil. Dip a few cauliflower florets at a time into the batter and then gently drop them into the hot oil. Fry in batches, flipping once during cooking until golden brown and crisp, 4–5 minutes per batch. If the oil starts smoking during the process, turn down the heat. Transfer to a kitchen paper-lined plate to drain and sprinkle lightly with salt, then transfer to a platter.

In a small bowl, whisk together 3 tablespoons full-fat natural yogurt and 1 tablespoon water. Drizzle the cauliflower with the yogurt and some of the pomegranate-lemon reduction. Sprinkle with ¼ teaspoon ground cumin, 3 tablespoons fresh pomegranate seeds and 1–2 tablespoons fresh chopped flat-leaf parsley. **Serves 4**

CRANAPPLE DOUBLE-GINGER RELISH

Yes, you can eat cranberries raw. When I was a kid, I used to dip them in sugar and pop them directly in my mouth. Admittedly, I was a bit of a strange child. But I stand by the idea: the crisp and airy texture of the berry mixed with sugar works – try it. I also add the raw berries to smoothies in the blender. For me, cooking cranberries has its place (compotes, pie filling, etc.), but using them raw shouldn't be overlooked. It allows them to retain their bite and inherent freshness. In general, I consider cranberries underrated – it's a shame people forget about them after Thanksgiving. Since cranberries are seasonal, I recommend buying the fresh berries in bulk and freezing them; they will last the year.

This sauce takes advantage of the zing of the fresh berries and fresh ginger. Mixed with the crisp sweet apple and mild sweetness of the brown rice syrup, it's a match made in heaven. You can make it with or without the nuts, but if you're a nut fiend like myself, the more the better.

Make about 550g (1lb 4oz)

50g (1¾oz) raw pecans
150g (5½oz) fresh cranberries
2 fresh apples such as Honey Crisp or Gala, peeled, cored and coarsely chopped (about 200g/7oz)
½ teaspoon grated fresh ginger
3 tablespoons brown rice syrup
2 tablespoons finely chopped crystallized ginger

1. Preheat the oven to 200°C (400°F), Gas Mark 6. Scatter the pecans on a baking sheet and place in the oven, tossing once halfway through cooking, until golden brown inside and toasted on the outside, 8–10 minutes. Let cool slightly, then coarsely chop.

2. Combine the cranberries, apples, grated ginger and brown rice syrup in a food processor and pulse about 40 times until finely chopped. Transfer to a medium bowl. Stir in the crystallized ginger and pecans until well combined. Serve immediately or store refrigerated in an airtight container for up to 1 week.

Extra Credit

● Spoon this relish on top of pancakes, waffles or **French toast** for a zippy alternative to maple syrup.

● Serve as a condiment alongside a **turkey and stuffing** dinner in place of cooked cranberry relish or sauce.

Homemade Granola and Yogurt Parfaits

To make the granola, preheat the oven to 160°C (325°F), Gas Mark 3. In a large bowl, combine 190g (6½oz) rolled oats, 25g (1oz) millet, 60g (2¼oz) coarsely chopped raw almonds and 70g (2½oz) raw, hulled pumpkin seeds (pepita). In a medium bowl, stir together 45ml (3 tablespoons) rapeseed oil, 2 tablespoons raw sesame seeds, 160g (5¾oz) brown rice syrup and ½ teaspoon salt. Pour the syrup mixture over the oat mixture and mix thoroughly to combine. (Store leftovers in an airtight container for up to 3 weeks.)

Spread the oat mixture out onto a parchment-lined baking sheet and bake, tossing a few times during the cooking process, until the granola is golden and crisp, 40–45 minutes. Transfer the sheet to a wire rack to cool completely.

Break up the granola into smaller chunks over a large bowl and stir in 65g (2¼oz) dried cherries, 70g (2½oz) sultanas and 70g (2½oz) pitted chopped Medjool dates.

To assemble the parfaits, spoon 55g (2oz) full-fat natural yogurt into the bottom of each of four parfait glasses and top with 55g (2oz) cranapple relish and a few tablespoons of the granola. Repeat the process twice, ending with the granola. Garnish each parfait with a fresh sprig of mint, if desired. **Serves 4**

● Top a slice of store-bought **Madeira** or **pound cake** with the sauce and a dollop of sweetened whipped cream.

● For an insta-snack, top a piece of toasted **rustic bread** or crackers with butter and the relish.

FIG AND BALSAMIC AGRODOLCE

Fond of figs? You're in luck because this recipe is based on fond and figs. Fond is culinary snob speak for the brown bits left over after you roast meat and vegetables. When scraped from the bottom of the pan, the fond (which in French literally means 'bottom') can be incorporated into a sauce, adding a ton of rich depth and caramelized goodness. To achieve the sublimity of this sauce, there is a prerequisite: it's based on your having already roasted some meat and/or vegetables in a frying pan. This could be beef, chicken and/or root vegetables – anything that can get nice and browned in the oven or on the hob. See the pork tenderloin recipe opposite for one suggestion.

Makes about 550g (1lb 4oz)

1 large heavy-bottomed frying pan with fond (see above)
2 tablespoons unsalted butter plus 2 tablespoons cold unsalted butter, cut into small pieces
25g (1oz) thinly sliced shallots
150g (5½oz) coarsely chopped dried figs, such as Mission or Turkish
1 tablespoon chopped fresh rosemary
120ml (4fl oz) balsamic vinegar
250ml (9fl oz) reduced-sodium chicken or beef stock

1. Drain any excess fat from the frying pan. Melt 2 tablespoons of the butter in the pan over a medium heat. Add the shallots and cook, stirring occasionally and scraping up any brown bits from the pan.

2. Continue to cook until the shallots begin to soften, about 3 minutes. Add the figs and rosemary and stir to combine. Add the balsamic, bring to a simmer and cook until the vinegar starts to thicken slightly, about 4 minutes. Add the stock and simmer until reduced slightly, about 10 minutes.

3. Turn off the heat and slowly whisk in the 2 tablespoons cold butter. Serve immediately.

Extra Credit

● Serve fig and balsamic agrodolce with pan-seared chicken or **lamb chops** instead of pork.

● Use as part of a **cheese plate**: my go-to cheeses to pair with this sauce are Parmesan, Gorgonzola dolce, Robiola and pecorino. Don't forget to serve nuts as well.

● Top a roasted **sweet potato** with some leftover sauce and a dollop of mascarpone.

● Cook sliced sausage, reserving the fond in the pan to make the sauce. Spread the sauce on **pizza** dough, sprinkle with the sausage and bake. Scatter with fresh rocket (argula).

Pan-Roasted Pork Tenderloin with Rosemary

Preheat the oven to 200°C (400°F), Gas Mark 6. Heat a large cast-iron or ovenproof heavy-bottomed frying pan over a medium-high heat. Season a room-temperature 550g (1lb 4oz) pork tenderloin all over with salt and pepper. When the pan is very hot, add 1 tablespoon olive oil and the pork and sear on all sides, about 6 minutes total.

Roast the pork in the pan until a meat thermometer inserted into the centre registers 60°C (140°F). Transfer the pork to a board to rest, covered loosely with foil, for about 10 minutes. Reserve the pan.

Slice the pork against the grain, drizzle with the fig and balsamic agrodolce sauce and garnish with more fresh rosemary leaves. Serve immediately or store the sauce refrigerated in an airtight container for up to 3 days. Bring to room temperature or rewarm slightly before using, taking care not to break the butter. **Serves 4**

DOWNRIGHT UPRIGHT APPLE SAUCE

When our daughter was just beginning to eat solid foods, I occasionally made my own baby food for her. One time, after making a much too large batch of apple sauce, I decided to spiff it up with some Calvados (apple brandy) and served it with cake and cream. Thus was born my spiked apple sauce. The alcohol is boiled off so you can feed this to youngsters if you wish (that's why I call it 'upright'). But the slightly floral fragrance of apples remains from the Calvados. I use a variety of apples to get a sweet and tart flavour combination. The versatile result is great eaten alone with a spoon, used as a yogurt topping, or as a condiment for roast pork tenderloin.

Makes about 950g (2lb 2oz)

120ml (4fl oz) apple cider
60ml (4 tablespoons) apple cider vinegar
2 tablespoons dark brown sugar
60ml (4 tablespoons) Calvados or other apple brandy
450g (1lb, about 2–3) Honeycrisp or Gala apples, peeled, cored and roughly chopped
450g (1lb) Golden Delicious apples, peeled, cored and roughly chopped
225g (8oz, about 1–2) Granny Smith apples, peeled, cored and roughly chopped

1. In a medium saucepan, combine the apple cider, vinegar, brown sugar and brandy and bring to the boil over a medium-high heat, about 4 minutes.

2. Stir in the apples, cover the pot and reduce the heat to medium-low. Cook until the apples are very soft, 20–25 minutes.

3. Use a potato masher to smash the mixture for a chunkier apple sauce; for a smooth texture, use a stick blender or transfer to a food processor and process until puréed. Let cool to room temperature, then transfer to the refrigerator to cool completely. Store refrigerated in an airtight container for up to 1 week.

Mashed Potato Pancakes with Soured Cream, Chives and Bacon

Peel 1.1kg (2lb 8oz) russet potatoes (about 3 large potatoes) and cut into 1cm (½in) pieces. Place in a large pot and add enough cold water to cover by 5cm (2in). Bring to the boil over a high heat and boil until the potatoes are tender, about 20 minutes total. Drain the potatoes, then press them through a ricer or smash them with a potato masher into a large bowl.

Let cool slightly, for about 10 minutes, then add 65g (2¼oz) plain flour, 2 large eggs, 2 teaspoons salt and ½ teaspoon black pepper and stir to thoroughly combine. Form the potato mixture into 8 equal-sized balls, then press each ball into a 10 x 2.5cm (4 x 1in) pancake and place on a parchment-lined baking sheet. Arrange three large shallow dishes or plates side by side. Fill one with 135g (4¾oz) plain flour, one with 2 beaten large eggs and one with 180g (6oz) panko breadcrumbs. Dip each pancake in the flour, then the eggs, then the breadcrumbs. Place each cake back on the prepared baking sheet and refrigerate until firm,

30 minutes–1 hour.
Meanwhile, cut 4 slices thick-cut bacon into 1cm (½in) pieces. Cook the bacon in a large high-sided frying pan, stirring occasionally, until crisp, about 5 minutes. Transfer the bacon to a kitchen paper-lined plate to drain, reserving the fat in the pan.

When the pancakes are chilled, reheat the pan over a medium heat. Add 1 tablespoon rapeseed oil and a few pancakes and cook for 6–8 minutes total, flipping them over halfway through cooking, until dark golden and crisp on both sides. Repeat with the remaining pancakes, adding more oil as needed. Transfer to a kitchen paper-lined plate to drain. Transfer to plates and top with dollops of soured cream, a large spoonful of downright upright apple sauce, fresh chopped chives and the crumbled bacon. Serve immediately. **Serves 4**

Nutty

The Mother Tahini . . . 88

Not As Slowly Mole . . . 90
[Baked Cheese Enchiladas]

Walnut and Sage Bagna Cauda . . . 92
[Roasted Whole Carrots with Labneh]

Thai Satay . . . 94
[Fresh Summer Rolls]

Poppy Seed and Parmesan Gloss . . . 98
[Orecchiette with Rainbow Chard and Breadcrumbs]

Golden Romesco . . . 100
[Marinated Grilled Calamari Kebabs]

Butternut Curry Cashew Cream . . . 102
[Tofu and Root Vegetable Stew]

Pistachio Crème . . . 104
[Crispy Salmon with Pea Greens]

The Mother Tahini

A staple of Middle Eastern cuisine, tahini is essentially sesame seeds ground into a paste. By itself it has a consistency similar to peanut butter. When you purchase it, you generally have to mix the oil and seed butter together, as they tend to separate in the jar. The flavour differs among brands; some might be slightly more bitter than others. I tend to like tahini on the milder side. To turn it into a sauce, you simply need to mix in some liquid and seasonings. It's just what you need atop a falafel or shawarma pita sandwich, but experiment a little and you will soon find a million other ways to use it.

Makes about 175g (6oz)

115g (4oz) tahini 2 tablespoons fresh lemon juice Sea salt	Whisk together the tahini, 90ml (6 tablespoons) hot water and the lemon juice in a medium bowl. Season to taste with salt. Use immediately or store in an airtight container in the refrigerator for up to 1 week (whisk again before using if oil from the sauce separates).

Mix It Up

Customize the mother sauce to your taste,
and to use in different ways.

  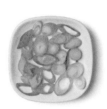 

Parsley, Carrot & Cumin Tahini

Stir in 70g (2½oz) finely grated fresh carrot, 10g (¼oz) chopped fresh flat-leaf parsley, and 1 teaspoon ground cumin.

Roasted Garlic, Coriander & Yogurt Tahini

Whisk in 8 chopped roasted garlic cloves, ½ teaspoon ground coriander (cilantro) and 55g (2oz) Greek yogurt or labneh (Middle Eastern strained yogurt).

Sesame Oil, Spring Onion & Soy Sauce Tahini

Stir in 1 teaspoon toasted sesame oil, 25g (1oz) thinly sliced spring onions and 4 teaspoons low-sodium soy sauce.

Honey, Vanilla & Black Pepper Tahini

Whisk in the seeds of 1 scraped vanilla pod, 3 tablespoons honey and a pinch of freshly ground black pepper.

Extra Credit

● Stir the honey, vanilla and black pepper tahini into yogurt and top with chopped nuts, dates and fresh fruit for an instant and **healthy breakfast**. Try it also drizzled on crisp apple slices.

● For at-home Chinese takeaway, toss the sesame oil, spring onion and soy sauce tahini with warm or cold **soba noodles**. Garnish with more spring onions and toasted sesame seeds.

●Serve the carrot, roasted garlic or mother tahini sauce with any grilled meat or chicken, especially in kebab form.

● For an easy side-dish salad, toss the carrot, garlic or mother tahini sauce with chickpeas, chopped parsley, chopped red pepper and **Israeli couscous**.

NOT AS SLOWLY MOLE

The Aztec word *mole* simply translates as 'mix'. This helps explain why the term is something of a catch-all for a large range of sauces. One thing that is almost always constant, though, is the inclusion of some sort of ground nut or seed. Making classic rich brown moles is typically a long and laborious process. Often they call for more than a dozen ingredients, many of which must be individually toasted, charred, sautéed, crushed and/or chopped by hand. This sweet and salty mole still has a long ingredient list, but it takes a fraction of the time of a traditional version. I usually eat it with roast chicken or turkey, but it also makes a lovely taco topping, burrito addition or sauce for enchiladas as in the recipe opposite.

Makes about 500ml (18fl oz)

1 tablespoon rapeseed oil
2 tablespoons raw flaked almonds
60g (2¼oz) chopped white onion
1 dried chilli, such as ancho or mulato, seeds and stem removed, torn or cut into small pieces
20g (¾oz) stale bread torn into small pieces
1 tablespoon raw sesame seeds
35g (1¼oz) raisins
2 garlic cloves, chopped
2 tablespoons raw hulled pumpkin seeds
375ml (13fl oz) low-sodium chicken stock
2 tablespoons roasted unsalted peanuts
¼ teaspoon ground cinnamon
½ teaspoon ground cumin
½ teaspoon ground coriander (cilantro)
6 tablespoons finely chopped dark chocolate
Sea salt

1. Heat the oil in a medium saucepan over a medium-high heat. Add the almonds and cook until just beginning to toast, about 4 minutes. Add the onions and cook, stirring occasionally, until soft, about 4 minutes.

2. Add the chilli, bread and sesame seeds and cook, stirring occasionally, until the seeds are lightly toasted, about 6 minutes. Add the raisins, garlic and pumpkin seeds and cook until fragrant, about 1 minute.

3. Pour in the chicken stock and bring the mixture to the boil over a high heat. Cook until the chilli softens, about 5 minutes.

4. Pour the stock mixture into a high-powered blender along with the peanuts, cinnamon, cumin, coriander and chocolate and blend until smooth. Season to taste with salt. Serve immediately or store refrigerated in an airtight container for up to 2 weeks.

Baked Cheese Enchiladas

Preheat the oven to 200°C (400°F), Gas Mark 6. Wrap twelve 13cm (5in) diameter corn tortillas in foil and warm them in the oven until pliable, about 15 minutes.

Meanwhile, grate about 280g (10oz) Monterey Jack cheese and set aside. Pour 250ml (9fl oz) of the mole into the bottom of an 20 x 20cm (8 x 8in) baking dish. Remove one tortilla at a time from the foil and top each with 2 tablespoons grated cheese.

Fold the tortilla in half and place in the baking dish. Repeat with the remaining tortillas and most of the cheese to form two overlapping rows.

Drizzle the tortillas with the remaining 250ml (9fl oz) mole and sprinkle with the remaining cheese. Cover the baking dish with foil, return to the oven and bake until the cheese has melted, about 15 minutes. Serve the enchiladas garnished with chopped white onion, coriander (cilantro) and fresh chopped avocado. **Serves 4**

The word 'chocolate' comes from the Aztec *xocolatl*, which translates as 'bitter water'. Mexicans have used unsweetened chocolate in savoury dishes for centuries (mole being the classic case). But Italians also took to the idea and use it in some pasta sauces.

WALNUT AND SAGE BAGNA CAUDA

Bagna cauda is a classic Italian sauce traditionally served warm and in the style of fondue with lots of veggies and bread to use as dipping agents. While the purist's version is made with garlic, olive oil and anchovies, my take, admittedly a very loose reinterpretation, uses browned butter, sage and walnuts. Serve it as a dip for veggies and crusty bread as you would the original. Or spoon this rich concoction over meat, fish or pasta. *Buon appetito!*

Makes about 125g (4½oz)

45g (1½oz) raw walnut halves
6 tablespoons unsalted butter
2 garlic cloves, chopped
2 tablespoons chopped fresh sage leaves
2 teaspoons fresh lemon juice
Sea salt

1. Preheat the oven to 200°C (400°F), Gas Mark 6. Scatter the walnuts on a baking sheet and place in the oven, tossing once halfway through, until golden brown inside and toasted on the outside, 8–10 minutes. Transfer to a food processor and pulse until finely ground.

2. Melt the butter in a medium saucepan over a medium heat. When the butter has melted, add the garlic and cook, stirring occasionally, until the garlic is fragrant and the butter takes on a nutty aroma, about 4 minutes. Stir in the sage leaves and turn off the heat. Stir in the ground walnuts and the lemon juice. Season to taste with salt. Serve warm.

Extra Credit

- Toss with **pasta** and some fresh rocket (arugula) and grated Parmesan cheese.

- Roast split **acorn squash**, fill the cavities with barley or farro and drizzle the sauce over all.

- Toss the sauce with cubed toasted bread, then toss with a beaten egg and just enough milk and/or stock to moisten; bake until crusty for a divine **bread stuffing**.

- Stir into plain cooked oats for a **savoury porridge** on a cold night.

Roasted Whole Carrots with Labneh

Preheat the oven to 220°C (425°F), Gas Mark 7. Cut off the leafy greens from 16 small to medium carrots and reserve for another use (such as in the carrot-top, kale and lemon pesto on page 51). Scrub any dirt off of the carrots. Place on a parchment-lined baking sheet and toss with 1 tablespoon olive oil, ½ teaspoon sea salt and ½ teaspoon freshly ground black pepper. Roast the carrots, tossing once or twice, until golden in parts, about 30 minutes. Remove from the oven and drizzle 1 tablespoon honey over the carrots. Return to the oven and continue to roast until golden brown and caramelized, about 5 minutes more.

Transfer to a serving plate. Drizzle with the bagna cauda, dollop with labneh (Middle Eastern strained yogurt) and top with a handful of fresh parsley leaves. Serve warm. **Serves 4**

THAI SATAY

When we order Thai food, we ask for extra peanut sauce but never seem to get as much as we want. So, when you can't beat them, join them: I started making my own. It is quite simple if you have the ingredients on hand and, luckily, most are pantry staples. A mixture of sweet, salty, creamy, slightly tart and spicy, this sauce lends itself to more flavourful cold crispy vegetables, hot grilled meats and noodles.

Makes about 500g (1lb 2oz)

1 tablespoon rapeseed oil
1 tablespoon finely chopped fresh ginger
1 medium shallot, finely chopped
1 garlic clove, finely chopped
225g (8oz) natural smooth peanut butter
1 tablespoon lime zest
60ml (4 tablespoons) fresh lime juice
50g (1¾oz) dark brown sugar
¼ teaspoon chilli flakes
2 tablespoons fish sauce

1. Heat the oil in a medium saucepan over a medium-low heat. Add the ginger, shallot and garlic and cook, stirring occasionally, until softened, about 4 minutes.

2. Add 175ml (6fl oz) water and bring to a simmer, about 2 minutes. Turn the heat off and stir in the peanut butter, lime juice, lime zest, brown sugar, chilli flakes and fish sauce until smooth. Serve at room temperature or store refrigerated in an airtight container for up to 1 week. Thin out with a couple of tablespoons hot water if necessary.

Use your imagination when it comes to the filling components of summer rolls. Think of the recipe opposite as just a blueprint. For instance, you could swap cooked shredded chicken breast for the prawns (shrimp), cooked sweet potato for the avocado, or cucumber for the cabbage.

Extra Credit

● For a splendid yet simple cold noodle salad, toss the peanut sauce with cooked and cooled **soba noodles**, chopped spring onions, shelled edamame and sesame seeds.

● Thin out the sauce with a few tablespoons of water and rice vinegar to turn into a peanutty **salad dressing**. Toss some with cucumbers, shredded Chinese cabbage, carrots and sliced raw mangetout.

● Roast spears of skin-on **sweet potato** until browned, then serve with the sauce for dipping.

● Thin with coconut milk, then simmer chicken thighs and cut-up potatoes in the sauce for an extra-rich **curry**.

Fresh Summer Rolls

Cook 85g (3oz) dried thin rice or mung bean vermicelli according to the packet instructions. Run under cold water and drain.

Place 16 cooked, peeled and deveined medium prawns (shrimp) on a board. Use a knife to slice each prawn in half horizontally. Place 10g (¼oz) fresh mint leaves; 55g (2oz) fresh coriander (cilantro) sprigs; 20g (¾oz) basil leaves; 1 pitted, peeled and thinly sliced avocado; 1 peeled, pitted and thinly sliced mango and 110g (4oz) shredded purple cabbage in separate piles or containers around your work surface. Fill a large shallow dish with very hot water. Ready 8 round rice wrappers, 25cm (10in) in diameter.

Working quickly with one wrapper at a time, completely submerge the wrapper in the water until it is soft and pliable, 10–15 seconds.

Remove the wrapper from the water and place on a board. Lay 4 prawn halves in a row, cut-side up, in the centre of the wrapper, leaving about 2.5cm (1in) of space on both sides. Top with a few slices of avocado, a few mint leaves, a couple of sprigs of coriander and basil leaves, a few slices of mango, 15g (½oz) cabbage and 35g (1¼oz) noodles. Fold the bottom half of the rice paper wrapper over the filling, then fold in the sides of the wrapper. Pressing down firmly, hold the folds in place and then tightly roll the wrapper up from bottom to top. Turn the roll over, seam-side down, so that the prawn faces up, and transfer to a large plate.

Repeat the process with the remaining 7 wrappers and filling ingredients and cover the plate with clingfilm (plastic wrap) until ready to serve. Serve at room temperature with a side of Thai satay for dipping.
Makes 8 rolls

POPPY SEED AND PARMESAN GLOSS

I love the light crunch and earthy flavour that poppy seeds bring to dishes. Occasionally someone in my cooking classes asks if poppy seeds are narcotic, knowing that opiates are derived from poppies. In a word, no. Opium is found in the pod of the poppy and not in the seed itself. So you can rest assured that any strange behaviour among your dinner guests cannot be blamed on this recipe. It will, however, offer plenty of less psychoactive delights. This is really the only sauce in the book that is based on a roux, a classic sauce-making technique.

Makes about 240g (8½oz)

3 tablespoons unsalted butter
2 garlic cloves, finely chopped
60ml (4 tablespoons) dry white wine
2 tablespoons plain flour
165ml (5½fl oz) low-sodium chicken or vegetable stock
1 tablespoon poppy seeds
25g (1oz) freshly grated Parmesan cheese
1 teaspoon fresh lemon juice
Sea salt and freshly ground black pepper

1. In a medium cast-iron or heavy-bottomed frying pan, melt the butter over a medium-low heat. Add the garlic and cook, stirring, until fragrant and softened, about 2 minutes. Pour in the wine, bring to a simmer and cook until reduced by about half, about 4 minutes. Whisk in the flour all at once and continue to cook and whisk for 2–3 minutes. Whisk in the stock and increase the heat to medium-high. Bring to a simmer, continuing to whisk until the sauce thickens.

2. Turn off the heat and stir in the poppy seeds, cheese and lemon juice. Season to taste with salt and pepper. Use immediately or store refrigerated in an airtight container for up to 1 week. To rewarm, place the gloss in a bowl over a pot of simmering water. Stir occasionally until warmed through.

Extra Credit

● Dress up plain **cooked beetroot** (or any root vegetable like young top-on carrots or steamed green beans) with this glossy sauce; it'll make them worthy of a dinner party.

● For an easy, hearty meal, add chopped toasted walnuts and fresh chopped parsley to the sauce and then toss with shredded rotisserie chicken and **kasha** (buckwheat groats) or boiled potatoes.

Orecchiette with Rainbow Chard and Breadcrumbs

Put a large pot of salted water onto a medium-high heat to boil. Wash and dry 550g (1lb 4oz) rainbow chard. Coarsely chop both the leaves and the stems separately.

Cook 450g (1lb) orecchiette in the boiling water until al dente according to the packet instructions. Meanwhile, warm 2 tablespoons olive oil in a large high-sided frying pan over a medium heat. Add 120g (4¼oz) freshly torn breadcrumbs and a pinch of salt and cook, stirring occasionally until golden, crisp and lightly toasted. Transfer to a small bowl.

Use kitchen paper to wipe out the pan and heat 3 tablespoons olive oil and 4 lightly smashed garlic cloves over a medium heat until the oil is fragrant and the garlic is golden brown, 2–3 minutes. Remove the garlic with a slotted spoon.

Raise the heat to medium-high and add the chopped chard stems. Season lightly and cook, stirring occasionally, until crisp tender and caramelized, about 5 minutes. Add the chopped chard leaves, 1 tablespoon lemon zest and a pinch of chilli flakes and toss until the leaves are wilted, 2–3 minutes.

Drain the pasta in a colander. Add the pasta and the poppy seed sauce to the pan and toss to combine with the chard. Season to taste. **Serves 4**

● Stir into **sautéed onions** and use as a topping for a bagel or toast for a snack

● Take frozen store-bought **pierogies** to a whole new level by coating them with this sauce.

GOLDEN ROMESCO

A rustic Catalonian sauce originally intended to go with seafood, romesco is a harmonious mélange of tomatoes, peppers, nuts, garlic and vinegar. The nuts, along with stale bread, not only add flavour, but thicken the sauce. It is generally red, but I love the sweetness that comes along with yellow tomatoes and yellow peppers; my romesco is not rust-coloured but golden.

Makes about 625g (1lb 6oz)

25g (1oz) flaked almonds
30g (1oz) rustic bread (cut or torn into 1cm/½in pieces)
1 large yellow pepper
550g (1lb 4oz) yellow tomatoes (2 large tomatoes)
5 tablespoons extra virgin olive oil
2 garlic cloves
1 tablespoon sherry vinegar
1 teaspoon sugar
½ teaspoon smoked paprika
Sea salt and freshly ground black pepper

1. Preheat the oven to 200°C (400°F), Gas Mark 6 with racks in the upper and middle levels. Spread out the almonds and bread pieces on a baking sheet, place on the middle oven rack and toast until lightly golden, 5–6 minutes. Transfer to a food processor and set aside.

2. Adjust the oven control to grill. Place the whole pepper and tomatoes on the same baking sheet that the almonds were toasted on. Rub the pepper and tomatoes with 1 tablespoon of the olive oil and grill on the upper oven rack, turning a few times during cooking until they are charred in parts, about 10 minutes.

3. Remove any stems and pepper seeds and transfer the peppers and tomatoes to the food processor along with the garlic, vinegar, sugar, paprika and remaining olive oil. Process until smooth, about 3 minutes. Season to taste with salt and pepper. Use immediately or store refrigerated in an airtight container for up to 1 week.

Extra Credit

● Steam **prawns (shrimp)**, red snapper and/or mussels. Transfer to a large serving bowl, spoon the sauce over the seafood and serve with plenty of bread.

● Smear golden romesco onto toasted rustic bread slices for an immediate **tapas** dish.

Marinated Grilled Calamari Kebabs

Soak eight 25cm (10in) skewers in a shallow pan of cold water for about 30 minutes before using. Rinse 550g (1lb 4oz) calamari tubes and tentacles, pat dry and cut into 5cm (2in) pieces.

In a medium bowl, whisk together 50ml (2fl oz) olive oil, 3 thinly sliced garlic cloves, 1 tablespoon freshly grated lemon zest, 2 tablespoons fresh lemon juice, 2 teaspoons chopped fresh oregano, 1 teaspoon chopped fresh thyme, 1 teaspoon salt and ½ teaspoon black pepper. Add the

calamari to the marinade, toss to combine, cover the bowl and refrigerate for about 30 minutes.

Preheat a grill or grill pan to a medium-high heat. Thread the calamari onto the skewers, discarding the marinade. Lightly oil the grill and grill the calamari on all sides until cooked through, 6–8 minutes total. Serve with a dish of the golden romesco for dipping and lemon wedges for squeezing. **Serves 4**

● Toss into cooked **pasta** along with shredded rotisserie chicken and baby spinach leaves for a quick and healthy dinner.

● Spoon over grilled **leeks** as a colourful summer side dish.

BUTTERNUT CURRY CASHEW CREAM

This recipe is my go-to when I want to eat healthy but still indulge in a little comfort food. So rich and thick it's almost a dip, I've dunked many a cracker in this stuff for a quick snack when I've been too lazy to cook. It's also completely vegan – shhh, don't tell. Oh and by the way, you can do this with other vegetables as well. A quick way to turn your veggies into a sauce.

Makes about 400g (14oz)

60g (2¼oz) raw cashews
280g (10oz) butternut squash, peeled, halved, deseeded and cut into 2.5cm (1in) chunks
2 x 2.5cm (1in) pieces fresh ginger
1 tablespoon extra virgin olive oil
Sea salt
½ teaspoon mild curry powder
½ teaspoon ground cumin
Freshly ground black pepper

1. Preheat the oven to 200°C (400°F), Gas Mark 6. Place the cashews in a small saucepan and cover by 5cm (2in) with cold water. Bring to the boil over a high heat, about 8 minutes. Turn off the heat, cover and let steep for about 35 minutes, until the cashews feel soft to the touch.

2. Meanwhile toss the butternut squash and ginger with the olive oil and ½ teaspoon salt. Spread out on a parchment-lined baking sheet and roast, tossing once or twice during cooking, until the butternut squash is cooked through and golden in parts, 30–35 minutes.

3. Drain the cashews, reserving 250ml (9fl oz) cooking liquid, and transfer to a high-powered blender or food processor along with the butternut squash mixture, the curry powder, cumin and the reserved cooking liquid. Blend on high speed for about 2 minutes, until smooth, rich and creamy. Season to taste with more salt and pepper.

Extra Credit

● Turn the sauce into a soup by warming **vegetable stock** in a saucepan and then stirring in the cashew cream to warm through.

● Mix some of the cashew cream with rice vinegar and olive oil to make a creamy salad dressing. Try this on sturdy greens like **chicory** or **endive** and/or kale massaged a few minutes with olive oil and salt.

Tofu and Root Vegetable Stew

In a large pot, heat 2 tablespoons olive oil over a medium heat. Add 2 finely chopped garlic cloves and 1 finely chopped shallot and cook, stirring occasionally, until fragrant, about 1 minute. Add 3 peeled carrots, 1 peeled russet potato, 1 peeled parsnip, 1 peeled sweet potato and 120g (4¼oz) 2.5cm (1in) pieces peeled swede. Stir in 150g (5½oz) trimmed and halved Brussels sprouts, 250ml (9fl oz) water and 1 teaspoon salt. Bring to a simmer, cover and cook until the vegetables are fork tender, about 10 minutes.

Remove the lid and add 140g (5oz) green beans cut into 5cm (2in) long pieces. Gently stir and return the lid to the pot. Cook until the green beans are tender but still green, about 10 minutes. Stir in the cashew cream and 250ml (9fl oz) water and heat through.

Gently stir in 400g (14oz) extra-firm tofu cut into 2.5cm (1in) cubes until heated through. Season to taste with salt and pepper. Serve with brown rice or another whole grain. Garnish with roughly chopped cashews and a squeeze of lime, if desired. **Serves 4**

● Add some chicken stock, cut-up cooked seasoned chicken breast and fresh herbs. Let simmer, then serve over **rice**.

● Use as a vegan alternative to mayo for a creamy **sandwich** spread.

PISTACHIO CRÈME

Word seems to have gotten around that we love pistachios in my household. As a result, every year around the holidays we receive multiple large bags of the roasted, salted, in-the-shell variety – about half a year's worth (no complaints here – keep 'em coming). While this kind of pistachio is ideal for snacking, for cooking purposes I often prefer to use raw nuts. They're on the expensive side, but you can buy only the amount you need. This rich and creamy savoury sauce has just the right amount of pistachio flavour and the airy texture creates a pillowy platform for anything from seafood to chicken to sit upon. It also makes a great vegan dip for crudités.

Makes about 250g (9oz)

110g (4oz) raw shelled pistachio nuts
2 tablespoons rapeseed oil
2 teaspoons sugar
1½ teaspoons white wine vinegar
Sea salt and freshly ground black pepper

1. Place the pistachios in a high-powered blender along with 250ml (9fl oz) boiling water. Let sit until the nuts begin to soften slightly, about 30 minutes.

2. Add the oil, sugar and vinegar and blend on high until smooth. Season to taste with salt and pepper. Use immediately or store refrigerated in an airtight container for up to 1 week.

Should you buy pistachios in the shell or shelled? Labour intensiveness notwithstanding, I'm a strong proponent of the former; you're more likely to end up with fresher-tasting, crunchier nuts.

Extra Credit

- Serve roasted sliced chicken breast in a pool of pistachio crème topped with **diced mango**, with coconut rice on the side. Toss with pasta, cooked prawns (shrimp) and asparagus for a satisfying meal.

- Pan-fry some **aubergine (eggplant)** slices until browned (breaded if you like), then top with a dollop of pistachio crème, fresh mint, pomegranate seeds and lemon zest for a tasty starter.

- Cut **pita bread** into triangles. Drizzle lightly with olive oil and sprinkle with sea salt, cumin, paprika and pepper. Bake at 200°C (400°F), Gas Mark 6 until crisp, then sprinkle with a bit of sumac. Serve along with the sauce as a dip.

Crispy Salmon with Pea Greens

Use kitchen paper to pat the skin dry on four 175g (6oz) pieces of centre-cut salmon (about 3cm/1¼in thick). Season all over with salt and pepper.

Heat a large cast-iron frying pan over a medium-high heat. When very hot, add 2 tablespoons rapeseed oil and swirl to coat the pan. Place the salmon, skin-side down, in the pan and cook without moving until the skin becomes golden brown and crisp, about 5 minutes. Flip the fillets and continue to cook until just cooked through, 3–4 minutes.

Meanwhile, heat 1 tablespoon olive oil and 1 tablespoon unsalted butter in a large high-sided frying pan over a medium heat. Add 310g (11oz) shelled peas to the pan and cook until warmed through, about 4 minutes. Add in 150g (5½oz) pea shoots and toss until just wilted, 2–3 minutes. Add 1 tablespoon fresh lemon juice to the pan, then season to taste with salt and pepper.

Use a spoon to spread 60g (2¼oz) of the pistachio crème onto the centre of each of four plates. Top each with the pea greens and one salmon fillet, skin-side up. Garnish with chopped pistachios, if desired. Serve immediately. **Serves 4**

Spicy

The Mother Chilli . . . 108

The Mother Chilli

To the uninitiated, cooking with dried chillies may seem daunting. Gazing at the shrivelled peppers in the package, you may ask, how in the world can these become a sauce? But once revived with a dip in a hot water bath and whizzed in a blender, the chillies undergo a miraculous transformation that makes the basis of this wonderfully silky sauce. Fresh and roasted chillies have their places, but nothing matches the flavour intensity of dried chillies. Chilli sauce, of course, has a million traditional uses within Mexican cuisine (see opposite for a few). But try it in other situations, too: Drizzle it on grilled sliced steak. Sauté prawns (shrimp) in the chilli, then use that to top cooked stone-ground grits or polenta. Or, fold a little into cooked long-grain rice and top with soured cream and chives for a side dish with extra zip.

Makes about 415g (14½oz)

4 mild to medium-hot dried chillies, such as ancho, Anaheim or mulato

60g (2¼oz) chopped white onion

2 garlic cloves, peeled

4 teaspoons agave nectar or brown sugar

2 tablespoons rapeseed oil

165ml (5½fl oz) low-sodium chicken stock, vegetable stock or water

2 teaspoons red wine vinegar

Sea salt

1. Cut the stems from the chillies. Remove the seeds and roughly chop or tear the chillies. Place them in the bowl of a blender or food processor along with 250ml (9fl oz) boiling water. Cover and let stand until softened, about 10 minutes.

2. Add the onion, garlic and agave and blend until smooth.

3. In a medium saucepan, heat the oil over a medium-high heat until shimmering. Add the chilli mixture and stir to combine. Pour in the stock. Bring to a simmer and cook, stirring occasionally, until thickened, about 8 minutes. Remove from the heat and stir in the vinegar. Season to taste with salt. Serve warm or room temperature. The sauce will keep refrigerated in an airtight container for up to 1 week.

Mix It Up

Customize the mother sauce to your taste,
and to use in different ways.

Creamy Lime Chilli

Stir in 2 teaspoons lime zest, 1 tablespoon fresh lime juice and 125g (4½oz) soured cream.

Sweet & Smoky Chilli

Stir in 1 teaspoon canned chipotles in adobo sauce, 1 teaspoon smoked paprika and 1 tablespoon honey.

Harissa Chilli

Stir in 1½ teaspoons ground coriander (cilantro), 2 teaspoons ground caraway and 2 teaspoons ground cumin.

Corn & Coriander Chilli

Stir in 140g (5oz) sweetcorn kernels, 3 tablespoons chopped fresh coriander and 1 teaspoon chopped fresh oregano.

Extra Credit

● For a party, slice a **quesadilla** into wedges on a plate. Serve with the chilli sauce in a ramekin in the centre for dunking. Or, pour some over tortilla chips on a baking sheet, top with grated cheese and bake – insta-nachos!

● Wrap warmed tortillas around a filling of your choice, then bathe them in this chilli sauce and bake until bubbling – **enchilada** night.

● For quick **chilaquiles**: Heat the sauce in a frying pan. Add a few large handfuls of tortilla chips and toss until the chips are well coated and start to soften slightly. Top with fried eggs and grated cheese.

● Simmer 450g (1lb) of lamb stewing meat in the harissa chilli until tender, adding water as needed to keep the meat almost submerged. Stir in a drained can of chickpeas. Serve with couscous or warmed tortillas for a **Mexi-Moroccan dinner**.

KOREAN BARBECUE

When I lived in LA, which has one of the largest Koreatowns in the US, one of my favourite things to eat out was Korean barbecue, or bulgogi. I discovered that what divides the commonplace from the exquisite is the quality of the sauce in which the meat or vegetables are marinated. While some bulgogi sauces incorporate raw onion and garlic that is then cooked along with the meat, this recipe requires pre-cooking the aromatics. This way you're not limited to using it as a marinade; you can also simply drizzle it over any cooked meat or seafood such as prawns (shrimp).

Makes about 500ml (18fl oz)

2 tablespoons rapeseed oil
80g (2¾oz) grated yellow onion
4 garlic cloves, finely chopped
2 tablespoons finely chopped jalapeño
2 teaspoons grated fresh ginger
35g (1¼oz) chopped spring onions, white and light green parts only
225g (8oz) ripe but firm Asian pear or Bosc pear, peeled and grated
6 tablespoons low-sodium soy sauce
60ml (4 tablespoons) rice wine or sake
60ml (4 tablespoons) mirin
25ml (1fl oz) toasted sesame oil
45g (1½oz) sugar
4 teaspoons gochujang
4 teaspoons fish sauce

1. Heat the oil in a medium saucepan over a medium-low heat. Add the onion, cover and cook until very soft, about 5 minutes.

2. Remove the lid and add the garlic, jalapeño, ginger, spring onions and pear and stir to combine. Raise the heat to medium and cook, stirring occasionally, until the pear softens, about 5 minutes.

3. Add the soy sauce, wine, mirin, sesame oil, sugar and gochujang, stir to combine and bring to a simmer, about 3 minutes. Pour into a food processor and process until smooth, about 2 minutes. Stir in the fish sauce. Let cool to room temperature before using as a marinade. Store refrigerated in an airtight container for up to 1 week.

Some bulgogi sauces are pretty mild, but mine has a kick due to the addition of jalapeño and gochujang, a fermented chilli paste.

● How about **baked beans** with a Korean twist for your next barbecue or picnic? Simmer (or bake) white beans in the sauce until thick and sticky.

● Whisk rice vinegar and rapeseed oil with a few tablespoons of bulgogi to turn it into a salad dressing. Try this with grated **daikon** for a kimchi-like starter.

● Grill **shiitake mushrooms**, then drape with this sauce. Cut into slices and serve as a starter.

● Brush **grilled pork tenderloin** with the sauce, then slice thinly across the grain. Serve in butter lettuce leaves with steamed cooled rice and drizzle with the sauce.

Beef and Kale Noodle Bowls

Wrap 450g (1lb) boneless beef rib-eye in baking parchment or clingfilm (plastic wrap) and place in the freezer for 1–2 hours, until just firm to the touch. Remove the paper and slice the meat across the grain into long, thin strips, about 2mm (¹⁄₁₆in) thick. (Alternatively, to save time, check your local Chinese market for pre-sliced rib-eye options.) Place the meat in a large bowl along with 3 peeled carrots cut into very thin matchsticks. Pour 375ml (13fl oz) Korean barbecue into the bowl with the beef and carrots. Toss to coat, cover and refrigerate for at least 30 minutes or overnight.

Cook 225g (8oz) noodles such as Korean guksu or Japanese udon according to the packet instructions. Run under cold water, then divide among four bowls.

Heat 1 tablespoon rapeseed oil in a large frying pan over a medium-high heat. Add half the beef and cook, stirring occasionally, until just cooked through, about 5 minutes. Transfer the meat to two of the bowls. Repeat the process with the remaining beef.

Wipe out the pan, then add 2 more tablespoons rapeseed oil, 300g (10½oz) chopped cavolo nero and 2 tablespoons toasted sesame oil and season to taste with salt. Use tongs to occasionally toss the kale over a medium-high heat until it is just wilted, about 4 minutes. Divide the kale among the bowls with the beef and noodles. Sprinkle each bowl with toasted sesame seeds and serve immediately.
Serves 4

NEW MEXICAN RED CHILLI

Love at first dip. That's how I'd describe my initial encounter with New Mexico-style chilli sauce. I was visiting my brother and future sister-in-law in Albuquerque and whenever we went to a restaurant, the same question popped up: do you want red or green chilli with that? I couldn't believe the flavour these sauces added to just about every dish. I love this sauce on eggs, hash browns and even prawns (shrimp).

Makes about 415ml (14½fl oz)

6–8 dried New Mexican red chillies
1 tablespoon rapeseed oil
1 tablespoon unsalted butter
60g (2¼oz) chopped white onion
2 garlic cloves, finely chopped
½ teaspoon ground cumin
½ teaspoon dried oregano
2 tablespoons plain or gluten-free flour
375ml (13fl oz) low sodium-chicken or vegetable stock
1 teaspoon honey
Sea salt and freshly ground black pepper

1. Remove the stems from the chillies, then rip them up into small pieces.

2. Warm the oil and butter in a medium saucepan over a medium heat. Add the chillies and onion and cook until the onion is translucent, about 2 minutes. Add the garlic, cumin and oregano. Cook, stirring constantly, until fragrant, about 1 minute. Stir in the flour and continue to cook for about 1 minute. Add the stock and bring to a simmer. Let cook, stirring occasionally, until the chillies have softened and the mixture thickens, about 12 minutes total.

3. Transfer to a high-powered blender or food processor along with the honey. Remove the middle part of the lid of the blender, if using, and cover with kitchen paper before blending to let the steam escape. Season to taste with salt and pepper. Serve warm or room temperature. Store refrigerated in an airtight container for up to 1 week.

Extra Credit

● Mix with mayo and use as a creamy spread for **sandwiches**, especially those featuring turkey.

● For a spicier green riff: substitute 40g (1½oz) dried Hatch green chillies for the red variety. Serve with a spinach and feta or queso fresco **omelette** or add a dollop to chicken and rice soup.

Fried Egg Tostadas

Preheat the oven to 200°C (400°F), Gas Mark 6. Line a baking sheet with baking parchment. Place four 13cm (5in) diameter corn tortillas on the prepared sheet and spread each with 3 tablespoons refried beans and 3 tablespoons Mexican grated cheese blend (spicy grated Cheddar as an alternative). Bake until the cheese has melted and the tortillas are crisp, 12–15 minutes.

Meanwhile, heat 2 tablespoons rapeseed oil in a large cast-iron frying pan over a medium-high heat. Crack 4 large eggs into the pan and season each with some salt and pepper. Cover with a lid and cook until the egg whites are set but the yolks are still runny, 6–8 minutes.

Transfer the tortillas to a plate and top with a fried egg, sliced avocado, coriander (cilantro) sprigs and a drizzle of New Mexican red chilli. Serve immediately. **Serves 4**

● Smear a large warm flour tortilla with the chilli, then top with refried beans, sweetcorn, rice, chopped tomatoes, avocado, soured cream and a squirt of lime. Roll up into a **burrito**.

● Drizzle over a **taco** in place of salsa, or bathe tortillas in it when making enchiladas.

GREEN COCONUT CURRY

In our household, we used to have a once-weekly ritual of ordering in Thai green curry. Then one day our local joint was closed and I decided to whip up my own. Curry is not a flavour in itself but a variable blend of aromatics and spices. My green curry relies slightly more on lemon grass than the typical Thai restaurant's, and it's a bit milder. If you want extra heat, just add more chilli. Toss this on any cooked protein and/or vegetables for a dinner you're sure to start craving weekly.

Makes about 500ml (18fl oz)

7.5cm (3in) piece fresh lemon grass, finely chopped
½–1 green Thai or Anaheim chilli, destemmed
1 tablespoon finely chopped fresh ginger
10g (¼oz) fresh basil leaves
15g (½oz) fresh coriander (cilantro)
½ shallot, chopped
2 garlic cloves
2 teaspoons fresh chopped makrut lime leaves
½ teaspoon ground coriander
½ teaspoon ground cumin
¼ teaspoon ground cardamom
4 teaspoons shrimp paste
3 tablespoons rapeseed oil
375ml (13fl oz) coconut milk
2 teaspoons palm sugar or dark brown sugar
4 teaspoons fish sauce
2 teaspoons fresh lime juice

1. In a food processor, combine the lemon grass, chillies, ginger, basil, coriander, shallot, garlic, lime leaves, ground coriander, cumin and cardamom and pulse about 50 times, until finely chopped. Add the shrimp paste and 2 tablespoons of the oil and process until a paste forms.

2. In a medium saucepan, heat the remaining 1 tablespoon oil over a medium heat. Add the green curry paste and stir constantly until simmering and heated through, about 3 minutes. Stir in the coconut milk, sugar and fish sauce. Bring to a simmer, about 4 minutes, and cook until the flavours develop, about 5 minutes. Turn off the heat and stir in the lime juice. Use immediately or store refrigerated in an airtight container for up to 1 week.

Extra Credit

● Add noodles and prawns (shrimp), chicken or tofu to the sauce for an easy dreamy noodle stew.

● Add 250–500ml (9–18fl oz) chicken or vegetable stock and a squeeze or two of fresh lime juice to make a soup base for **gai tom ka soup**.

● Drizzle green coconut curry over cooked beef or **chicken skewers**, or use as a marinade for skewered meat before grilling.

● Revive **leftover rice** by simmering it in this curry; top with meat, vegetables and fresh herbs.

Sizzling Thai Mussels

Scrub 1.8kg (4lb) fresh mussels well and cut off the beards. In a large bowl, toss the mussels in 1 tablespoon rapeseed oil. Heat a large tall pot with a lid over a medium-high heat. When very hot, add the mussels. Use a long spoon to stir a few times as they sizzle in the pot. Add the green coconut curry, reduce the heat to medium, stir to combine and cover with the lid. Cook, stirring once or twice, until the mussels have opened, 10–12 minutes.

Transfer the mussels and sauce to a serving dish, discarding any unopened mussels. Garnish with fresh torn basil leaves. Serve immediately. **Serves 4**

ETHIOPIAN BERBERE SAUCE

If you haven't yet tried the vibrant and highly flavourful cuisine of Ethiopia, I'd urge you to seek it out. The basis of most meals is a tangy, spongy flatbread called injera. Many different types of stewed dishes are placed in little piles atop the bread. Diners tear off pieces of injera to scoop up the meats and vegetables – utensil-free eating. This spicy sauce is my way of making the most of berbere, the famous dried spice mix that comes from Ethiopia. Berbere brings new life to any cooked vegetable or as a marinade for beef or chicken. I also use it as a condiment for grilled meats and bread.

Makes about 315ml (11fl oz)

1 teaspoon fenugreek seeds
¼ teaspoon ground allspice
2 green cardamom pods
⅛ teaspoon freshly grated nutmeg
⅛ teaspoon ground cinnamon
¼ teaspoon cayenne pepper
½ teaspoon black peppercorns
3 tablespoons extra virgin olive oil
1 medium onion, finely chopped
2 tablespoons finely chopped fresh ginger
1 tablespoon finely chopped fresh turmeric or 1 teaspoon ground turmeric
4 garlic cloves, finely chopped
120ml (4fl oz) dry red wine
20g (¾oz) finely chopped fresh coriander (cilantro)
1 teaspoon red wine vinegar
1 teaspoon sea salt

1. Using a mortar and pestle or a spice grinder, grind the fenugreek, allspice, cardamom, nutmeg, cinnamon, cayenne pepper and black peppercorns together and set aside.

2. Heat the oil in a medium saucepan over a medium heat. Add the onion, ginger and turmeric and cook, stirring occasionally, until the onion is very soft, about 15 minutes.

3. Add the garlic and dried spice mixture and cook until fragrant, about 1 minute, then pour in the wine and cook until almost completely evaporated, about 4 minutes. Turn the heat off and stir in the coriander, vinegar and salt. Serve warm or room temperature. Store in an airtight container in the refrigerator for up to 1 week.

- Stir a bit of sauce into rice and cooked minced beef, then use as a filling for baked **stuffed red peppers**.

- Stir the sauce into cooked **lentils** and serve with rice, or if you have it, injera.

- Amp up a classic supper of the American South: Stir the sauce into stewed **spring greens** and serve with cornbread for dunking.

- Spread a bit of sauce onto toasted rustic bread, then top with **sliced roast beef**, avocado, tomato, microgreens and another piece of toasted rustic bread.

Winter Squash and Chickpea Stew

Heat 45ml (3 tablespoons) extra virgin olive oil in a large high-sided frying pan over a medium-high heat. Add 675g (1lb 8oz) 2.5cm (1in) pieces of winter squash (from either 1 small butternut, kabocha or acorn). Cook, stirring occasionally, until tender and golden brown in parts, about 20 minutes.

Add 425g (15oz) drained cooked chickpeas and 1 teaspoon salt and cook, stirring occasionally, until the chickpeas are warmed through, about 3 minutes. Stir in 60g (2¼oz) tomato purée until completely combined, then stir in 1 batch Ethiopian berbere and 250ml (9fl oz) water,

reduce the heat to medium-low and simmer to develop the flavours, about 3 minutes.

Season to taste with more salt. Serve warm or room temperature with a dollop of full-fat yogurt, a handful of fresh coriander and pita, naan or injera if you can find it in a speciality shop. **Serves 4**

When using fresh herbs, don't discount the stems; they have tons of flavour. If they're tender, chop and add along with the leaves to your sauces and other recipes. If they're woodier, save them in a large resealable container in the freezer, to throw into stock.

CHARRED POBLANO AND TOMATILLO MOJO

This lovable mutt of a recipe incorporates elements of Mexican, Caribbean and Southwestern cooking. For a sauce with such complexity (sweet, tart, spicy, creamy, salty all in one!) it is relatively simple to make. A few brief notes on ingredients: The tomatillo, a diminutive and tart relative of the tomato that you eat when still green, has a thin papery husk you must remove. While poblano peppers generally range from mild to medium heat, once in a while you end up with a spicy one. If you want even more heat, add a jalapeño to the mix when grilling the vegetables. If you want more creaminess, stir in some soured cream. My instinct is to use this sauce on tacos, but don't let that stop you from experimenting with other options.

Makes about 750ml (1⅓ pints)

2 poblano peppers
4 medium tomatillos, husks peeled
1 medium white onion, peeled and cut into quarters
3 garlic cloves, unpeeled
2 tablespoons rapeseed oil
1 avocado, pitted and peeled
3 tablespoons fresh lime juice
20g (¾oz) chopped fresh coriander (cilantro)
Sea salt

1. Preheat the grill with a rack position at the highest level. Toss the poblanos, tomatillos, onion and garlic in the oil and spread out on a baking sheet. Grill the vegetables, tossing a few times during the process, until blistered all over, 8–10 minutes.

2. Transfer just the poblanos to a medium bowl. Cover the bowl with clingfilm (plastic wrap) and steam the peppers for about 10 minutes. Peel and seed the poblanos and transfer them to a food processor along with the tomatillos, onion, peeled garlic and avocado. Pulse until smooth. Add the lime juice, coriander and salt to taste and pulse to combine. Store refrigerated in an airtight container for up to 1 week.

Extra Credit

● How about green eggs (ham optional)? Serve the mojo over **fried eggs** on toast for a real wake-up breakfast.

● For an island-style feast, grill some **red snapper** fillets, then spoon this sauce on top. Serve with the smashed plantains oposite and/or black beans and rice on the side.

● Tired of the same-old guacamole? This sauce will turn any bag of **tortilla chips** into a party.

● Drizzle over **fried aubergine** (see page 59), or almost any fried veggie really.

Crispy Smashed Plantains

Cut the ends off each of 3 green plantains. Use a knife to make a vertical slit down each one, then carefully peel the plantains and slice crossways into 2.5cm (1in) thick slices.

Pour 2.5cm (1in) of rapeseed oil into a large high-sided frying pan and heat over a medium-high heat until a deep-fry thermometer reads 182°C (360°F). Fry the plantains in batches (turning over once halfway through cooking) until lightly golden, about 4 minutes per batch. Use a slotted spoon to transfer the plantains to a kitchen paper-lined baking sheet. Turn off the heat.

Use a heavy metal spatula or meat mallet to smash the plantains to 5mm (¼in) thickness. Reheat the oil to 182°C (360°F). Fry the plantains again in batches until dark golden and crisp, about 4 minutes. Return to the kitchen paper-lined baking sheet and immediately sprinkle with salt. Dip the plantains in the charred poblano and tomatillo mojo and serve immediately.

Serves 4

AUBERGINE ZHOUG

This bright green Middle Eastern sauce, especially popular in Yemen and Israel, is summertime in a bowl, often served atop a pita sandwich or shawarma. Typically, zhoug is a smooth and spicy pesto-like condiment. Mine is chunkier since it uses chopped grilled aubergine (eggplant) as the base. When mixed with hot peppers, fresh herbs, olive oil and spices, it livens up toast or crackers, gives sandwiches a flavour boost and adds a kick to a grilled steak.

Makes about 500ml (18fl oz)

550g (1lb 4oz) aubergine (eggplant), peeled and sliced crossways into 5mm (¼in) thick rounds
5 tablespoons extra virgin olive oil
1–2 jalapeños, stems removed
25g (1oz) fresh coriander (cilantro) leaves and stems
25g (1oz) fresh flat-leaf parsley leaves and stems
10g (¼oz) fresh mint leaves
1 garlic clove, peeled
½ teaspoon ground coriander
½ teaspoon ground cumin
4 teaspoons red wine vinegar
1 teaspoon dark brown sugar
Sea salt and freshly ground black pepper

1. Preheat a grill or grill pan to a medium-high heat. Brush the aubergine with 2 tablespoons of the olive oil. Lightly oil the grill and cook the aubergine in batches for 6–8 minutes, flipping halfway through cooking, until grill marks form on both sides. Transfer the aubergine to a board, roughly chop into approximately 5mm (¼in) pieces and place in a medium bowl.

2. In the bowl of a food processor, combine the jalapeños, coriander, parsley, mint, garlic, ground coriander, cumin, vinegar, sugar and remaining olive oil and pulse about 30 times, until finely chopped. Add to the bowl with the aubergine and gently stir to combine. Season to taste with salt and pepper. Store refrigerated in an airtight container for up to 5 days.

Extra Credit

● Spoon onto toasted flatbread for a Middle Eastern twist on **bruschetta** and serve with olives.

● Stir aubergine zhoug into **cold pasta** for a pasta salad that will transport you to the Mediterranean.

Spiced Socca with Feta

In a medium bowl, whisk together 95g (3¼oz) chickpea flour, ¾ teaspoon salt, ½ teaspoon black pepper, ¼ teaspoon smoked paprika and ½ teaspoon ground coriander. Whisk in 175ml (6fl oz) warm water and 2 tablespoons extra virgin olive oil until smooth. The batter should be the consistency of double cream. Cover the bowl with clingfilm (plastic wrap) and let sit for about 1 hour.

Preheat the oven to 260°C (500°F), Gas Mark 10. Place a 25cm (10in) cast-iron frying pan in the oven to heat. Remove from the oven once hot, add 2 tablespoons olive oil to the pan and swirl to coat. Pour the batter into the pan and return to the oven. Cook until the socca is firm and set and the edges are golden brown, 12–15 minutes.

Turn out the socca onto a board and cut into wedges. Spoon some of the aubergine zhoug over the top and sprinkle with 3 tablespoons crumbled feta and a bit of za'atar. Serve immediately. **Serves 4**

● Top a round of **pizza** dough with cheese and thawed frozen artichoke hearts. Bake in a hot oven until crispy, then spoon the aubergine zhoug on top.

● Make a fabulous **veggie sandwich** starting with good-quality multigrain bread, then top with aubergine zhoug, tahini sauce (page 88), fresh basil, tomato slices, roasted red peppers, grated carrots and chopped lettuce.

QUICK JERK

This recipe is inspired by an airport meal, believe it or not. My husband and I were taking a trip to the Caribbean island of Tortola – with multiple stops thanks to a shoestring budget. After travelling all day, we finally arrived, parched and starving, at what might be called an airport, although it was really little more than a strip of land between two huge gorgeous mountains overlooking the bright aqua ocean. We stumbled over to the café – a straw-thatched cottage with outdoor seats and many cats and goats milling around. The menu was simple . . . jerk chicken, jerk goat and a couple of side dishes. I went with the chicken (the goats staring at us made it an easy choice). The dish that arrived was revelatory: freshly grilled, deliciously charred, flavourful to the bone, and so juicy yet crisp on the exterior. It was the best meal of our entire trip, despite many other good ones. I have thought about that meal many times since, though it was almost ten years ago. My version of the jerk sauce – a pretty fair approximation if I may say so – uses lots of aromatics including freshly grated nutmeg. A purist would insist on chopping by hand but this quick jerk uses the help of a food processor to speed things along. I like to use it as a marinade or simmer it and spoon it on top of grilled seafood or meat.

Makes about 330g (11½oz)

4 spring onions, chopped
115g (4oz) chopped white onion
4 teaspoons chopped fresh ginger
2 garlic cloves, peeled
½–1 Scotch bonnet or jalapeño chilli
1 tablespoon fresh thyme leaves
4 teaspoons tomato purée
2 tablespoons dark brown sugar
2 tablespoons lime zest (from 2 limes)
1½ teaspoons ground allspice
½ teaspoon freshly grated nutmeg
5 tablespoons fresh lime juice
1 tablespoon rapeseed oil
1½ teaspoons sea salt
½ teaspoon freshly ground black pepper

Place all of the ingredients in a food processor and process for about 2 minutes, scraping down the sides of the bowl, if necessary, until a paste forms. Use immediately or store refrigerated in an airtight container for up to 2 weeks.

Extra Credit

● Jerk is really just barbecue sauce, Caribbean style. Use it anywhere you might use barbecue sauce, such as atop a **burger**.

● For a quick dip, beat 2-3 tablespoons quick jerk into 115g (4oz) cream cheese and 60g (2¼oz) soured cream and stir in chopped spring onions. Use as a **dip** for any raw vegetables and /or crackers.

● Brush some onto **corn on the cob** right before it goes on the grill.

● For a vegetarian take on jerk, stew canned **jackfruit** in some of the sauce until the flavours marry. Serve with rice and peas.

Double Jerk Chicken Wings

Place 1.25kg (2lb 2oz) chicken wings or party-style wings in a large resealable bag with 250g (9oz) of the quick jerk. Press out the air from the bag, seal and use your hands to press and move the bag around to coat the wings in the sauce. Let marinate in the refrigerator for at least 1 hour.

Preheat the oven to 240°C (475°F), Gas Mark 9. Transfer the chicken wings to a large bowl and toss with 3 tablespoons plain flour and ½ teaspoon salt. Arrange the wings on an oil-rubbed parchment-lined baking sheet and bake, flipping once halfway through cooking, until they are browned in parts, cooked through and crisp, 35–40 minutes.

Meanwhile, place the remaining 80g (2¾oz) jerk sauce and 120ml (4fl oz) water in a small saucepan over a medium heat. Bring to a simmer and cook until the mixture has thickened, about 15 minutes. Remove the chicken from the oven and brush the cooked sauce over the top. Transfer the wings to a serving platter and garnish with fresh chopped spring onions. Serve immediately. **Serves 4**

KIMCHI BUTTER

This sauce has only four ingredients but packs a flavour wallop nonetheless, thanks to its two primary ingredients, kimchi and koji (see Notes). Both of these products can usually be found at Korean markets or purchased online. If you can't find koji, try substituting sweet white miso, which has a similar flavour. While kimchi is typically eaten cold, here I've warmed it and added butter to mellow out the intensity, and the richness of the koji further rounds out the flavour. I like eating this sauce stirred straight into steamed white or brown rice. It's also superb as a topping for starchy sides, as in the recipe opposite.

Makes about 190g (6½oz)

1 tablespoon unsalted butter, plus
4 tablespoons cold unsalted butter,
cut into small pieces
45g (1½oz) mild to medium
kimchi, chopped
2 teaspoons shio rice koji
or sweet white miso
½ teaspoon rice vinegar

Melt 1 tablespoon of the butter in a medium saucepan over a medium heat. Add the kimchi and cook until heated through, about 3 minutes. Stir in the shio koji and vinegar and turn off the heat. Whisk in the remaining 4 tablespoons cold butter, a little at a time, until the sauce thickens. Serve immediately.

Note: Kimchi, as you may know, is a Korean fermented condiment made of fermented raw vegetables (usually Chinese cabbage), garlic, ginger, chillies, salt and vinegar. I absolutely love the flavour and texture and heat.

As for koji (full name shio koji), this is a fermented white paste made of malted rice, salt and water, which adds a rich umami flavour that enhances anything it touches.

Extra Credit

● Use in place of butter for a more flavourful **baked potato** topper to serve alongside a classic steak meal.

● Stir kimchi butter into rice or any **whole grain** and top with a fried egg and some shredded toasted seaweed for a comforting meal.

Seoul Crispy Rice Cakes

In a large bowl, combine 250g (9oz) cooked and cooled steamed white rice, 70g (2½oz) grated raw carrot, 45g (1½oz) grated raw courgette (zucchini), 20g (¾oz) chopped spring onions, 2 teaspoons toasted sesame oil, 2 teaspoons low-sodium soy sauce, 1 tablespoon glutinous rice flour (mochiko) and ½ teaspoon salt. Beat 1 large egg in a small bowl and stir it into the rice mixture. Form the rice mixture into eight 6cm (2½in) diameter cakes. (The mixture will feel loose.) Place the patties on a parchment-lined baking sheet and refrigerate for 1 hour, or until firm.

Heat 2 tablespoons rapeseed oil in a large high-sided frying pan over a medium-high heat. Once shimmering, add the rice cakes in batches. Cook, flipping once during the cooking process, until golden brown and crispy on both sides, about 4 minutes total per batch. Drain on a kitchen paper-lined plate, then transfer to plates and spoon kimchi butter over the top. Serve immediately. **Serves 2-4**

● Stir kimchi butter into sautéed mixed vegetables such as kale, chopped sweet potatoes and **kohlrabi** and serve on top of buckwheat soba noodles with a splash of soy sauce and sesame oil.

● Spoon onto a store-bought puffed **rice cake** for a flavourful snack.

Chunky

The Mother Salsa . . . 128

The Mother Salsa

Salsa simply means 'sauce' in Spanish. So it makes sense that Mexican salsas vary considerably in texture and ingredients. In general, though, our north-of-the-border definition of salsa revolves around a base of fresh veggies or fruits, diced or blended, with some form of heat, citrus or vinegar, plus aromatics and salt. Here I've concentrated on the fresh and chunky variety (if you are a fan of blended hot sauces, take a look at the Mother Chilli on page 108). Pretty much any of these work as a chip dip, burrito component or taco topper.

**Makes about
500g (1lb 2oz)**

250g (9oz) chopped ripe tomatoes
60g (2¼oz) chopped white onion
10g (¼oz) chopped fresh coriander (cilantro)
2 tablespoons fresh lime juice
1 tablespoon deseeded and finely chopped jalapeño
Sea salt

Place the tomatoes, onion, coriander, lime juice and jalapeño in a medium bowl and stir to combine. Season to taste with salt. Let sit at room temperature for up to 30 minutes for the flavours to develop. Use right away or store refrigerated in an airtight container for up to 3 days.

Mix It Up

Customize the mother sauce to your taste,
and to use in different ways.

Pineapple & Chipotle Salsa

Replace the tomatoes with 215g (7½oz) chopped fresh pineapple. Replace the jalapeño with 1 tablespoon chopped chipotles in adobo.

Sweetcorn & Roasted Garlic Salsa

Stir in 70g (2½oz) cooked fresh sweetcorn kernels, 6 chopped roasted garlic cloves (see Note) and ½ teaspoon ground coriander (cilantro).

Avocado & Mango Salsa

Replace the tomato with 325g (11½oz) chopped fresh mango and stir in 70g (2½oz) chopped fresh avocado and ½ teaspoon chilli powder just before serving.

Apple & Radish Salsa

Replace the tomatoes with 100g (3½oz) chopped Granny Smith apple and 6 chopped radishes and replace the white onion with 60g (2¼oz) chopped red onion.

Note: To roast garlic: Preheat the oven to 200°C (400°F), Gas Mark 6. Cut about 1cm (½in) off the top of 1 head of garlic, exposing a little of the cloves, and place on a piece of foil on a baking sheet. Pour 2 tablespoons extra virgin olive oil over the top of the garlic and then wrap in the foil. Roast until the garlic cloves are very tender and slightly golden, 45–50 minutes.

Extra Credit

● For a quick snack, fill half of a **pitted avocado** with any one of the salsas (except the avocado one). Eat with a spoon.

● Use the pineapple and chipotle or avocado and mango variations to top **grilled fish** or prawns (shrimp).

● Beautifully accessorize **gazpacho** or a chilled avocado soup with any of these salsas.

● Make a weekday pork chop dinner special by serving with the apple and radish salsa, maybe with some **polenta** or grits on the side.

BACON AND CHIVE GALLIMAUFRY

Gallimaufry means a hodgepodge, confused medley, ragout or hash. Its etymology seems rooted in old French words for 'have fun' and eat copious quantities. I came up with this recipe because of, well, bacon. The other ingredients complement the bacon's natural richness, adding notes of sweetness and acidity. It is great just slapped onto some bread or used as a topper for a creamy winter squash or root vegetable soup. The uses are endless if you are craving bacon, which, let's face it, you probably are.

Makes about 190g (6½oz)

4 slices thick-cut bacon, coarsely chopped
1 medium shallot, finely chopped
60ml (4 tablespoons) apple cider
3 tablespoons apple cider vinegar
1 teaspoon dark brown sugar
2 tablespoons cold unsalted butter, cut into small cubes
3 tablespoons snipped fresh chives
Sea salt and freshly ground black pepper

1. Cook the bacon in a medium cast-iron or heavy-bottomed frying pan over a medium heat, stirring occasionally, until fat has rendered and the bacon is crisp. Use a slotted spoon to transfer the bacon to a kitchen paper-lined plate. Reserve the fat in the pan.

2. Add the shallot to the pan and cook, stirring occasionally, until it just begins to soften, about 3 minutes. Add the cider, vinegar and brown sugar and cook until reduced by half, about 4 minutes. Whisk in the butter, a few pieces at a time, until it melts and the sauce takes on a glossy consistency. Stir in the bacon and chives and season to taste with salt and pepper. Use immediately.

Extra Credit

● This makes a lovely warm dressing for any number of sturdy **salad greens**, such as spinach, rocket (arugula), frisée or kale.

● Spoon gallimaufry over **cooked scallops**, prawns (shrimp) or clams to launch them into the flavour stratosphere.

● Spread on a piece of **toast** and top with a fried egg for a sophisticated twist on bacon and eggs.

● If you want something a little more virtuous to balance out all the butter and bacon, toss this sauce with some roasted **cauliflower florets**.

Whipped Turnip Mashed Potatoes

Peel 450g (1lb) turnips and 900g (2lb) russet potatoes. Cut both into 4cm (1½in) pieces and place in a large pot. Pour in enough cold water to cover the potatoes and turnips by 5cm (2in). Season with 2 tablespoons salt. Bring the water to the boil over a high heat, about 15 minutes. Continue to boil until the root vegetables are fork tender, about 8 minutes. Drain and return to the pot. Use a ricer or potato masher to mash them together.

In a separate small saucepan, combine 150ml (5fl oz) double cream, 3 tablespoons unsalted butter, 90ml (6 tablespoons) chicken or vegetable stock, 1 bay leaf and 3 sprigs fresh thyme. Bring to the boil over a medium heat and continue to cook until the flavours develop, about 3 more minutes. Discard the bay leaf and thyme and pour the liquid over the root vegetable mixture.

Use a spoon to combine and season to taste with salt. Transfer the turnip potatoes to a serving dish and pour the bacon and chive gallimaufry over the top. Serve immediately. **Serves 4**

SALSA AL COURGETTES

From my days in cooking school, I remember a chef instructor discussing the difference between French and Italian cuisines. In French cuisine, the raw ingredients tend to get manipulated and transformed into something new and wonderful – a silky soufflé or a wobbly terrine. Italian cooking, in contrast, seeks to showcase and emphasize the natural flavours and textures of the ingredients being used. I love both styles, but this summery recipe goes the Italian route. Briny pancetta, juicy tomatoes and fresh courgettes (zucchini) shine as the key ingredients. A few notes on them: 1) If you can find them, I recommend using small courgettes in this recipe as their flavour tends to be more delicate than large late-summer courgettes, which can become woody (save these for courgette bread). 2) The tomatoes are added at the end along with the herbs, after the heat has been turned off. This warms them through without cooking them, allowing you to maintain their fresh and juicy quality and avoid mushiness. The fresher the better. 3) The pancetta, a salty cured pork, is more of a supporting player than star in this dish – its primary purpose is to enrich the vegetables in the sauce. The end result is a coarsely chopped, rustic sauce that's great with pasta or as a topping for grilled or roast chicken.

Makes about 875g (1lb 15oz)

85g (3oz) pancetta, cut into small dice
3 garlic cloves, thinly sliced
2 small courgettes (about 350g/12oz total), cut into 1cm (½in) dice
2 chopped ripe tomatoes (about 350g/12oz total)
1 tablespoon balsamic vinegar
20g (¾oz) torn basil leaves
10g (¼oz) chopped fresh parsley
Sea salt and freshly ground black pepper

1. Heat a large high-sided frying pan over a medium-high heat. Add the pancetta and cook, stirring occasionally, until the fat has rendered and the pancetta is crisp, 2–3 minutes.

2. Add the garlic to the pan and cook, stirring occasionally, until fragrant, about 1 minute.

3. Add the courgettes and cook, stirring constantly, about 3 minutes, until crisp tender. Turn the heat off and add the tomatoes, vinegar, basil and parsley. Toss to combine and season to taste with salt and pepper. Serve immediately.

Extra Credit

- Top **pizza** dough (store-bought or homemade) with the sauce and fresh mozzarella or Parmesan. Bake until the cheese has melted, the sauce is bubbly and the crust is golden.

- Halve an **acorn squash** lengthways, roast until tender, then top with this sauce for a healthy dinner.

- Make a **prawn-and-rice** Italian stir-fry: After cooking the salsa in the pan, toss in some prawns, (shrimp) season with salt and pepper and cook until the prawns are just opaque, 2–3 minutes. Then stir in 250g (9oz) pre-cooked rice and toss through until warm.

- Use as a **polenta** topping for a quick but satisfying meal.

Ricotta and Herb Gnocchi

Place 350g (12oz) full-fat ricotta in a large bowl. Add 1 large egg, 40g (1½oz) grated Parmesan cheese, 1 tablespoon extra virgin olive oil, 10g (¼oz) finely chopped flat-leaf parsley, 2 teaspoons chopped fresh thyme leaves, 1 teaspoon salt and ½ teaspoon black pepper and stir to combine. Add 175g (6oz) plain flour and stir until a dough forms.

Turn out the dough onto a lightly floured large board. Form into a ball, adding more flour if the mixture feels too sticky. Cut the ball into 4 equal pieces, then roll each into a 1cm (½in) thick rope. Cut crossways into 2.5cm (1in) pieces. Roll each piece off the back of the tines of a fork to make imprints. Place on a parchment-lined baking sheet.

Bring a large pot of salted water to the boil. Add half the gnocchi and cook until they have floated to the top of the pot, about 3 minutes. Repeat the process with the remaining gnocchi.

Transfer the gnocchi to the frying pan with the salsa al courgettes. Add 2 tablespoons extra virgin olive oil and toss to combine. Serve immediately, sprinkled with more Parmesan cheese, if desired. **Serves 4**

KALEIDOSCOPE CHICKPEA AND TOMATO HASH

This extra-chunky medley of a sauce was designed to appeal equally to the palate and the palette (thank you very much, I'll be appearing in Cleveland tomorrow!). It provides a colourful, painterly backdrop and a creamy, mellow richness to whatever it accompanies. Its centrepiece, the humble chickpea, brings a hit of protein and satisfying heft that, combined with a platform grain or pasta, makes for a legit main course. This sauce is a real scene stealer, in a good way, since it brings so much to the table that you can pair it with the blandest of foods, from leftover green beans to turkey breast. Or, for a killer app, simply smother it on some thinly sliced rustic toast and top with mozzarella.

Makes about 500g (1lb 2oz)

45ml (3 tablespoons) extra virgin olive oil
3 garlic cloves, thinly sliced
1 tablespoon chopped fresh rosemary
1 tablespoon tomato purée
140g (5oz) cooked or canned chickpeas, rinsed and drained
330g (11½oz) halved small cherry or grape tomatoes of any colour
120ml (4fl oz) low-sodium chicken or vegetable stock
2 tablespoons chopped fresh flat-leaf parsley
Sea salt and freshly ground black pepper

1. In a large high-sided frying pan, warm the olive oil and garlic over a medium-low heat, stirring occasionally. When the garlic begins to look lightly golden around the edges, about 6 minutes, add the rosemary and tomato purée and stir to combine.

2. Add the chickpeas and stir gently to combine and warm through. Add the tomatoes and stock. Raise the heat to medium-high, bring to a simmer and cook until the tomatoes have softened slightly, about 3 minutes. Stir in the parsley and season to taste with salt and pepper. Use immediately or store refrigerated in an airtight container for up to 3 days.

Extra Credit

- Fill crêpes with the sauce, fold over to form triangles, top with grated **Gruyère cheese**, then bake in the oven until the cheese is melted.

- In a baking dish coated with olive oil, layer thinly sliced aubergine (eggplant) and courgettes (zucchini) with the sauce and mozzarella cheese. Cover with foil and bake until cooked through for a gluten-free, **pasta-free lasagna** (as on page 60).

Roast Chicken Thighs Provençal

Preheat the oven to 230°C (450°F), Gas Mark 8. Pat 6 bone-in, skin-on chicken thighs dry with kitchen paper and season all over with salt and pepper. Heat a large cast-iron or heavy ovenproof frying pan over a high heat. When very hot, add 1 tablespoon rapeseed oil and half the chicken, skin-side down, to the pan. Let cook, undisturbed, until the skin is crisp and golden brown, about 4 minutes. Flip over and continue to cook until browned on all sides, about 4 more minutes.

Transfer the chicken, skin-side up, to a plate. Drain the fat from the pan and repeat with the remaining chicken. Take the pan off the heat and drain all the fat from the pan.

Pour the chickpea and tomato hash into the pan and bring to a simmer over a medium heat, about 4 minutes. Place the chicken thighs on top of the sauce and transfer to the oven. Continue to roast until the thighs have an internal temperature of 74°C (165°F), 15–18 minutes. Remove from the oven and let rest for 5 minutes before serving. Divide among plates and top with freshly torn basil leaves. **Serves 4 as a small plate**

● Fold the sauce into cooked **couscous**, maybe with some briny black olives for a main-course salad that will really sparkle at a picnic.

● Slice **focaccia** in half, spoon on the chickpea and tomato hash, top with a fried egg and you have an exemplary sandwich.

OLD SCHOOL BROOKLYN HOT SALAD

Deep into Brooklyn, there is a fabled sandwich shop known as Defonte's. We used to make the trek for their coronary-inducing heroes, overflowing with meat, sometimes several kinds within a sandwich. One of their famous sides is a combo of pickled veggies known as 'hot salad'. Not really a salad, and not that hot either, this relishy sauce hearkens back to a time when Italian-American cuisine was still trying to position itself in a way that the mainstream could understand. What follows is my riff on it.

Makes about 625g (1lb 6oz)

1 mild light green chilli, such as Hungarian wax
1 red pepper
3 garlic cloves, unpeeled
3 tablespoons plus 1 teaspoon extra virgin olive oil
60g (2¼oz) pimento-stuffed green olives
50g (1¾oz) pitted Kalamata olives
2 pepperoncini, stems removed
2 tablespoons drained capers
1 tablespoon red wine vinegar
25g (1oz) chopped fresh flat-leaf parsley

1. Preheat the grill with a rack on the highest level. Toss the mild green and red peppers and the garlic in 1 teaspoon of the oil and spread out on a baking sheet. Grill the vegetables, tossing a few times during the process, until blistered all over, 8–10 minutes. Transfer the peppers to a medium bowl, cover the bowl with clingfilm (plastic wrap) and steam for about 10 minutes. Peel and deseed both peppers and place in the bowl of a food processor. Peel the garlic and add it to the food processor along with the olives and pepperoncini. Pulse about 15 times, until coarsely chopped. Transfer to a medium bowl.

2. Add the capers, vinegar, parsley and remaining 3 tablespoons olive oil and stir to combine. Use immediately or refrigerate in an airtight container for up to 4 days. Bring up to room temperature about 30 minutes before using.

Extra Credit

● Sprinkle the sauce over a bowl of store-bought **hummus** and you have a starter worthy of a mezze platter.

● Slice an aubergine (eggplant) and roast until light golden. Let cool slightly. Place a spoonful of Brooklyn hot salad in the middle of each slice, roll them up and secure with toothpicks to create **involtini**.

Super Italian Hoagie

Split two 30cm (12in) Italian loaves in half lengthways. In a small bowl, mix 60g (2¼oz) tomato purée with 2 tablespoons olive oil. Spread on the bottom half of each loaf. Evenly spread some of the Old School Brooklyn hot salad over the tomato purée.

Top each sandwich with 70g (2½oz) thinly sliced mortadella, 40g (1½oz) thinly sliced salami, 70g (2½oz) thinly sliced capicola (coppa), 70g (2½oz) thinly sliced provolone cheese, 50g (1¾oz) shredded iceberg lettuce, 1 thinly sliced ripe tomato and 5–6 fresh basil leaves.

Spread a thin layer of mayo on the top half of each loaf and close the sandwiches. Slice each sandwich in half crossways and serve immediately. **Serves 4**

● Top mild, grilled fish with the old school hot salad and serve with **Tenderstem broccoli (broccolini)** and blistered tomatoes alongside.

● Stir a little into canned **olive oil–packed tuna** for a great mayo-free tuna salad option.

QUINCE, APPLE AND TURMERIC CHUTNEY

I first tried quince when I was on my honeymoon in coastal Uruguay. In South America the fruit most commonly appears in a Spanish preparation called membrillo, in which it's cooked into a jelly-like paste that is often served as part of a cheese course. The membrillo was deliciously tart, sticky and sweet, acting to break the richness of all the salty and creamy cheeses. Upon my return to the United States, I immediately added quince to my flavour arsenal. Similar in shape and appearance to a pear, the quince must be cooked to be eaten; after a while on the heat its light yellow flesh turns a darker amber. The quince's core is very hard and contains inedible seeds; use a good sharp knife to carefully remove it. This chutney, which incorporates apples and fresh spices like ginger and turmeric to contrast with the quince, is perfect for any cheese plate or as a condiment for a variety of meats and sandwiches – try it mixed with mayo when used in a chicken salad sandwich.

Makes about 1.1kg (2lb 8oz)

1 teaspoon rapeseed oil
1 teaspoon mustard seeds
1 teaspoon cumin seeds
115g (4oz) chopped yellow onion
1 tablespoon finely chopped fresh ginger
2 tablespoons finely chopped fresh turmeric or
1 tablespoon ground turmeric
1 teaspoon ground coriander (cilantro)
½ teaspoon ground cardamom
2 large quinces, peeled, cored and coarsely chopped
90ml (6 tablespoons) apple cider vinegar
100g (3½oz) dark brown sugar
2 apples, such as Gala or Honeycrisp, peeled, cored and coarsely chopped
70g (2½oz) sultanas
1 teaspoon salt

1. Warm the oil in a medium saucepan over a medium heat. Add the mustard seeds and cumin seeds and cook, stirring constantly, until toasted, about 30 seconds.

2. Add the onion and cook, stirring occasionally, until soft, about 5 minutes. Stir in the ginger and turmeric and cook until just fragrant, about 2 minutes. Stir in the coriander and cardamom to combine.

3. Add the quince, 120ml (4fl oz) water, the vinegar and brown sugar, and stir to combine. Bring to a simmer, cover and cook, stirring once or twice, until tender, about 10 minutes. Stir in the apples, cover and simmer until the apples are tender, about 10 minutes. Stir in the sultanas and salt. Let cool to room temperature, then refrigerate in an airtight container for up to 2 weeks.

- For an out-of-this-world **grilled cheese**, lacquer one side of the bread with this chutney, layer with thin-sliced ham, then Cheddar and toast in a frying pan with lots of butter on both sides.

- Whisk 2 tablespoons of chutney with oil and vinegar; toss with chopped roasted root veggies like parsnips and carrots, spinach, pumpkin seeds (pepita) and pumpernickel croutons for a splendid **autumn salad**.

- The rarity of quince makes them perfect for a holiday table. Serve this chutney alongside **roast ham** or turkey instead of, or in addition to, cranberry sauce.

- For a sweet and savoury side, top a baked **sweet potato** with this chutney, soured cream and chopped bacon.

Toast with Raclette and Watercress

Preheat the oven to 200°C (400°F), Gas Mark 6. Slice two 1cm (½in) thick slices from 1 loaf of rustic bread. Place the bread on a baking sheet in the oven until lightly toasted, 6–8 minutes. Transfer the toast to two plates.

Cut 140g (5oz) Raclette cheese into 1cm (½in) cubes. In a medium cast-iron or nonstick frying pan, heat the cheese cubes just until melted, then continue to cook, stirring once or twice, until the cheese starts to stick slightly to the bottom of the pan and becomes melted and bubbly, about 8 minutes total.

Top both pieces of toast with some of the melted cheese, scraping up and including any sticky bits, then top each serving with 75g (2½oz) quince, apple and turmeric chutney and a handful of watercress. Serve immediately. **Serves 2**

If you're a jammer, don't throw away the cores and peels of quince. They are packed with pectin. Freeze them so you can later simmer with water for a homemade pectin solution that will help firm up any number of preserves.

GRILLED ARTICHOKE TAPENADE

While tapenades are generally olive based, here olives are usurped by artichokes, which bring a similar umami flavour and meaty texture. This recipe is inspired by the artichokes at a special little place called Caputo's in Brooklyn. It was there I first encountered artichokes *sotto olio* (preserved in olive oil). As a California native I'd enjoyed artichokes my whole life, but I had never had anything like these: large bulbs grilled over a wood fire, partially blackened, and so deliciously smoky and earthy. This recipe uses frozen artichoke hearts which, when grilled, do a surprisingly good job of simulating the Caputo's experience and forming the basis for this flavour-packed, rustic sauce.

Makes about 625g (1lb 6oz)

350g (12oz) packet frozen, thawed and drained artichoke hearts
5 tablespoons extra virgin olive oil
1 tablespoon plus 1 teaspoon fresh lemon juice
2 garlic cloves, finely chopped
1 tablespoon lemon zest
2 tablespoons drained capers
10g (¼oz) chopped fresh flat-leaf parsley
Sea salt and freshly ground black pepper

1. Preheat a grill or grill pan to a medium-high heat. In a medium bowl, toss the artichoke hearts with 2 tablespoons of the olive oil and 1 tablespoon of the lemon juice and season with ¼ teaspoon salt and ¼ teaspoon pepper. Working in batches if necessary, cook the artichokes on the grill, flipping them halfway through, until grill marks form on all sides, about 6 minutes total. Transfer to a large board and, when cool enough to handle, coarsely chop and return to the bowl.

2. Warm the remaining 3 tablespoons olive oil and the garlic in a small frying pan over a medium heat. When the garlic begins to soften and is fragrant, stir in the lemon zest and capers. Pour the olive oil mixture over the artichokes. Stir in the parsley and remaining teaspoon of lemon juice. Season to taste with salt and pepper. Serve warm or room temperature. Store refrigerated in an airtight container for up to 1 week.

Extra Credit

- Stir the tapenade into brown rice, along with peas, broad beans, baby spinach and radishes for a **spring rice salad**.

- Toss artichoke tapenade with **penne rigate**, chopped grilled chicken and pea shoots; eat it warm or room temperature.

Pan Bagnat

Slice four 10cm (4in) square ciabatta rolls in half crossways. Tear out some of the soft bread from the inside of each half (save the scraps for breadcrumbs or to feed the birds). Divide 2 drained 140g (5oz) cans tuna packed in olive oil among the bottom halves of each roll.

Top with thinly sliced seedless cucumber, thinly sliced tomatoes, thinly sliced red onion and 4 thinly sliced hard-boiled eggs. Season to taste with salt and pepper. Then top with fresh basil leaves and the artichoke and lemon tapenade.

Wrap each sandwich tightly in clingfilm (plastic wrap) and place them under something heavy, such as a heavy pot or cast-iron pan, until slightly pressed, about 30 minutes. Unwrap each sandwich and slice in half. Serve immediately or within 2–3 hours. **Serves 4**

● Rub slices of grilled sourdough or rustic bread with raw garlic, then top with some of the tapenade for a quick and easy **bruschetta**.

● Create a breadless bruschetta for your gluten-free friends by spooning the tapenade into little romaine or butter **lettuce boats**.

Chunky   143

NIBLETY CORN RELISH

I've never been to the Deep South, but it's on my bucket list, primarily because of the food. When I lived in Brooklyn, I had a friend from New Orleans named Karina who taught me how to fry fish and cook okra. Corn relish is a traditional Southern condiment with sweet, vinegary qualities that cut through all that delicious, indulgent fried Southern fare. When developing this recipe, I played around with the proportions until I achieved my goal: a condiment that tastes like a sweetcorn pickle. It is a great counterpoint to rich fried foods such as fried chicken or fish, as it adds a bright and tangy flavour that cuts through the grease. I even like eating it plain.

Makes about 500g (18oz)

2 teaspoons rapeseed oil
2 tablespoons finely chopped shallot
1½ teaspoons yellow mustard seeds
1 bay leaf
35g (1¼oz) finely chopped red pepper
35g (1¼oz) finely chopped green pepper
280g (10oz) fresh sweetcorn kernels or thawed frozen sweetcorn
5 tablespoons white wine vinegar
3 tablespoons sugar
Sea salt

1. Heat the rapeseed oil in a medium saucepan over a medium heat. Add the shallot, mustard seeds, bay leaf and red and green peppers. Cook, stirring occasionally, until the shallot has softened, about 4 minutes.

2. Add the sweetcorn and toss to combine. Add the vinegar and sugar and bring to a simmer, stirring occasionally. Season to taste with salt.

3. Let cool to room temperature, then discard the bay leaf. Use immediately or store refrigerated in an airtight container for up to 1 week.

Extra Credit

● Trick out a **lobster roll** with this relish instead of the usual butter and celery salt. Or add it to your arsenal of hot dog or sausage toppings.

● Spoon on top of **fried green tomatoes**.

● For a vintage-style starter, spread whipped **cream cheese on top of crackers** and top each with a small spoonful of niblety corn relish.

● Brighten up a pot of stewed **pinto beans** by using this sauce as a topper. In the Appalachians, this makes a fine supper along with a wedge of cornbread.

Polenta-Crusted Trout

Whisk 60ml (4 tablespoons) full-fat milk and 2 large eggs in a large shallow dish. Season with 1¼ teaspoons salt and ½ teaspoon black pepper. In a separate shallow dish, combine 190g (6½oz) finely ground polenta with 1 teaspoon salt and ½ teaspoon black pepper.

Dip four 115g (4oz) boneless skin-on trout fillets into the egg mixture, then coat well on both sides in the polenta and place on a parchment-lined baking sheet.

Heat 3 tablespoons rapeseed oil in a large cast-iron or heavy-bottomed frying pan over a medium-high heat. When hot, add the fillets in 2 batches if necessary and cook each batch until golden brown and crisp on both sides, 2–3 minutes per side. Transfer the fish to four plates and spoon the corn relish on top. Serve immediately.

Serves 4

8

Confectionery

The Mother Ganache

Ganache is simply a fancy word for what you get when you stir chopped chocolate into hot double cream until the two come together. Its uses are endless. Warm, it can be drizzled onto cakes or ice cream, or used as a dunker for shortbread or biscotti. Cooled in the refrigerator, it can serve as a decadent spread on toast, used to fill cookie sandwiches, scooped to make a soft truffle filling, or even get whipped into a delectable chocolate icing. Stir a few tablespoons into hot milk for fancy hot chocolate. Just make sure to buy the best-quality chocolate – I like Scharffen Berger or Callebaut – and equally good cream, since these ingredients are the stars.

Makes about 215g (7½oz)

115g (4oz) good-quality 62% chocolate
150ml (5fl oz) double cream
1 tablespoon unsalted butter, cut into small pieces

1. Use a large serrated knife to finely chop the chocolate and place it in a medium heatproof bowl.

2. Bring the cream just to the boil in a small saucepan over a medium-high heat, 3–4 minutes, then turn off the heat. Pour the cream over the chocolate and let rest for 5 minutes.

3. Add the butter and stir until the butter is melted and the chocolate is smooth. Serve immediately or store refrigerated in an airtight container for up to 1 week. To reheat, bring the ganache to room temperature, then transfer to a large metal bowl and place on top of a pot of simmering water to create a bain-marie. Stir until warm and smooth.

Mix It Up

Customize the mother sauce to your taste,
and to use in different ways.

Passion Fruit Ganache	Aztec Ganache	Vegan Coconut & Almond Masala Ganache	Salted Malted Ganache
Substitute 115g (4oz) 70% dark chocolate for the 62% chocolate. Stir in 60g (2¼oz) fresh passion fruit pulp with seeds (from 3 passion fruits) and 2 tablespoons passion fruit liqueur.	Stir in ½ teaspoon chilli powder, ½ teaspoon cinnamon and 1 teaspoon pure vanilla extract.	Replace the cream with 165ml (5½fl oz) full-fat coconut milk. Omit the butter and stir in 55g (2oz) smooth almond butter. Stir in ¾ teaspoon garam masala.	Substitute 115g (4oz) milk chocolate for the 62% chocolate. Whisk 25g (1oz) malted milk powder into the hot cream and stir in ½ teaspoon sea salt.

Extra Credit

● Peel a **banana**, freeze it on a stick, then dip into the passion fruit variation. Let it set until the chocolate is firm. A tropical paradise.

● Fold an equal amount of smooth **peanut butter** into the ganache and refrigerate until firm. Scoop out spoonfuls and roll into balls for a treat that's better than store-bought peanut butter cups.

● **Fondue** parties aren't just for cheese: Make it a dessert party with a big pot of this sauce, or better yet, one of each variation, along with a smorgasbord of fresh and dried fruits and biscotti for dipping.

QUÉBÉCOIS MAPLE BUTTER

When my husband first tried this sauce his eyes popped out of his head like a Warner Brothers cartoon character and, moments later, he was using his finger like a rubber scraper to frantically wipe up every molecule from the plate. Think of it as maple syrup on steroids – the butter, cream and salt result in an alchemical concoction that tastes like liquefied maple sugar candy. Recommended for bears pre-hibernation, or anyone who could use some comfort against the cold.

Makes about 325g (11½oz)

260g (9½oz) pure maple syrup
115ml (3¾fl oz) double cream
4 tablespoons cold unsalted butter, cut into small pieces
½ teaspoon sea salt

1. Bring the maple syrup and cream to the boil in a medium saucepan over a medium-high heat, about 4 minutes. Continue to cook, stirring occasionally, until bubbling and slightly thickened, about 5 minutes.

2. Whisk in the butter and salt. Serve warm or room temperature. Store refrigerated in an airtight container for up to 2 weeks. Bring to room temperature or rewarm in a bowl set over a water bath.

Extra Credit

● For **cinnamon toast** fit for a queen, spread this maple butter on thick sourdough slices, let it sink in a minute, sprinkle with cinnamon and bake until crispy at the edges.

● Pour over the top of a **Bundt cake** for instant icing.

● Revive day-old banana bread, **gingerbread**, or just about any quick bread by toasting slices then drizzling this sauce over the top.

● Pour over fresh-popped **popcorn** for a sweet-and-salty treat.

Polenta Crêpes

In a high-powered blender, combine 135g (4¾oz) plain flour, 100g (3½oz) finely ground polenta, ½ teaspoon salt, 1 tablespoon sugar, 440ml (15½fl oz) room-temperature full-fat milk, 2 large room-temperature eggs and 3 tablespoons melted and cooled unsalted butter and blend until a smooth batter forms. (It should be the consistency of double cream.) Let it sit at room temperature for about 30 minutes.

In a small bowl, combine 2 tablespoons rapeseed oil and 2 tablespoons melted unsalted butter. Heat an 20cm (8in) crêpe pan or heavy-bottomed frying pan over a high heat for about 2 minutes, until very hot, turn off the heat and let sit for about 2 minutes. Then reheat the pan to medium and brush with some of the oil and butter mixture. Pour 4 tablespoons batter onto the pan and swirl to evenly coat. Cook until bubbles form in the middle, about 2 minutes. Use a spatula to carefully flip the crêpe over and continue to cook, about 1 minute more. Transfer to a baking sheet or plate. Repeat the process until all the batter has been used. Divide among plates and drizzle with the Québécois maple butter. **Makes eleven 20cm (8in) crêpes**

MATCHA WHITE CHOCOLATE

I bought a tin of matcha (green tea powder) on a whim a while ago, in truth because the packaging was so pretty. Naturally, it sat in the cupboard untouched for months. I finally decided to do something about the lonely container and thus was born Matcha White Chocolate. Think of the silky texture of chocolate sauce, but much more delicately flavoured with (and tinted by) green tea. Creamy and comforting, this pourable sauce might also be even a tiny bit healthy due to the green tea (just humour me). A jar of this sauce makes a great hostess present; the pale jade colour invariably elicits oohs and aahs. In fact I think it may even be prettier than that original tin.

Makes about 150ml (¼ pint)

115g (4oz) white chocolate
225ml (8fl oz) double cream
2 teaspoons matcha powder
Pinch of sea salt

1. Finely chop the white chocolate and place in a medium bowl.

2. Whisk the cream and matcha powder in a small saucepan until combined. Over a medium heat, bring to a simmer, about 4 minutes. Begin whisking again as the mixture comes to the boil and continue until it is very smooth, about 2 minutes.

3. Pour the hot matcha cream over the chocolate. Let sit for about 5 minutes. Whisk until smooth, then whisk in a pinch of salt. Use warm or at room temperature.

Extra Credit

● Top a bowl of berries with a scoop of vanilla **ice cream** and drizzle with this sauce for a colourful variation on a summer sundae.

● Transform a plain bakery-bought **cheesecake** into something spectacular by spreading a thin layer of this sauce on top.

● Stir into **rice pudding** and sprinkle more matcha on top.

● How about a symphony in green? Serve over **pistachio cake** and garnish with mint leaves.

Matchaccino

In a medium saucepan, warm 250ml (9fl oz) full-fat milk and 250g (9oz) evaporated milk over a medium heat until just simmering, about 8 minutes.

Transfer the milk mixture to a high-powered blender along with 1 batch warm matcha white chocolate and blend until frothy, about 2 minutes.

Pour into mugs and serve garnished with fresh whipped cream and a sprinkle of matcha powder, if desired. **Serves 4**

KATIA'S CREAMY VANILLA ELIXIR

I developed this custard sauce, similar to a crème anglaise, in honour of our daughter, Katia. She will eat anything, just as long as it is white. While I can count the meals she will tolerate on one hand, she loves to help me in the kitchen and I always reward her by putting a little pure vanilla extract on her wrists like perfume. Hence Katia's Creamy Vanilla Elixir: warm, creamy and sweet with lots of vanilla flavour (and free of any colours that might distract your palate). This sauce is a puffy cloud of pure comfort. Serve with warm chocolate anything, from cake to soufflé – for that matter, drizzle it on almost any dessert. But if you're serving it to fancy company, take care not to lick the spoon.

Makes about 500ml (18fl oz)

1 vanilla pod
120ml (4fl oz) full-fat milk
340ml (10½fl oz) double cream
2 large egg yolks
45g (1½oz) sugar
1 teaspoon cornflour
1 tablespoon cold unsalted butter, cut into small pieces
1 teaspoon pure vanilla extract
Pinch of sea salt

1. Use a sharp knife to make a vertical slit down the length of the vanilla pod and place it in a medium saucepan along with the milk and cream. Bring to a simmer over a medium-low heat, stirring occasionally, 12–15 minutes.

2. Meanwhile, whisk together the egg yolks, sugar and cornflour in a medium bowl until pale yellow and smooth but thick.

3. Slowly pour the cream mixture, a ladleful at a time, into the egg yolk mixture while whisking constantly to temper the egg yolks.

4. Pour the mixture back into the saucepan and continue to cook over a medium heat, stirring constantly until simmering and thickened, 8–10 minutes. Turn off the heat and whisk in the butter, vanilla and salt.

5. Pour the sauce through a fine-mesh sieve into a clean medium bowl and let cool slightly. Serve warm or place clingfilm (plastic wrap) directly on the surface of the sauce to prevent a skin from forming and refrigerate until cool. At this point, you may transfer to an airtight container and store, refrigerated, for up to 3 days.

● Serve **angel food cake**, Madeira or pound cake and fresh berries over a pool of Katia's creamy vanilla elixir.

● Blend with milk, bananas and ice cubes for a thick and creamy milkshake. This is great if you want a **milkshake** but don't have ice cream around.

● For grown-ups only: blend the elixir with full-fat milk, nutmeg and rum for a riff on **eggnog**.

● Drizzle on **pears** poached in wine sauce.

Pear, Apple and Cardamom Tart

Thaw 1 sheet from a 475g (1lb 1oz) packet puff pastry according to the packet instructions. Lightly sprinkle a work surface with plain flour and place the puff pastry on top. Lightly flour the pastry and roll it out into a 30 x 35cm (12 x 14in) rectangle. Transfer to a parchment-lined baking sheet and place in the refrigerator for about 15 minutes to firm up. Preheat the oven to 200°C (400°F), Gas Mark 6.

Peel 2 Golden Delicious apples and 2 ripe but firm Bosc pears. Use a sharp knife to thinly slice them into 5mm (¼in) thick slices. Place the apples in one medium bowl and the pears in another. Toss each with 1 teaspoon fresh lemon juice, 1½ tablespoons sugar, ¼ teaspoon ground cardamom and a pinch of salt.

Alternating pear and apple, arrange the fruit slices close together and overlapping in four rows on top of the dough, leaving a 2.5cm (1in) border around the edges. Dot the fruit with 1 tablespoon butter cut into small pieces.

Fold the edges in over the fruit to create a 1cm (½in) dough rim. Pinch the four corners to seal the dough. In a small bowl, beat 1 tablespoon water with 1 egg. Brush the egg wash on the rim and sprinkle the rim with 1 tablespoon sugar.

Bake until the puff pastry is deep golden brown and the fruit is cooked, 35–40 minutes. Let cool slightly before slicing the tart into 8 slices. Serve warm or room temperature drizzled with the vanilla elixir. **Makes one 30 x 35cm (12 x 14in) tart; serves 8**

COCONUT AND LEMON GRASS INFUSION

Lemon grass is a long and stalky perennial herb usually grown in warm and tropical climates. Originally from India but used with great frequency in Southeast Asian cooking, it has a lovely, distinctive, fresh, zingy aroma. Being quite fibrous, it is best to think of lemon grass not so much as an ingredient to use raw on its own, but as an herb that flavours something else. This can be achieved either by finely chopping the less fibrous part and adding it to a dish, or by steeping it in water or a syrup to create an infusion, as is done here. This recipe combines the bright notes of lemon grass with the richness of coconut milk. The result is a sauce that allows you to make over a wide range of desserts, such as the kebabs opposite, with a tropical flavour profile.

Makes about 335ml (11½fl oz)

4 fresh lemon grass stalks
45g (1½oz) sugar
120ml (4fl oz) full-fat coconut milk
160g (5¾oz) sweetened condensed milk
2 tablespoons fresh lime juice
2 teaspoons lime zest
¼ teaspoon sea salt

1. Tear off any dried outer leaves from the lemon grass, cut off the stem ends and finely chop. You should have about 60g (2¼oz). Combine the chopped lemon grass, sugar and 60ml (4 tablespoons) water in a medium saucepan. Bring to the boil over a medium heat, stirring until the sugar has dissolved. Turn off the heat, cover the pan and steep until the syrup is very fragrant, about 1 hour.

2. Pour the mixture through a fine-mesh sieve into a medium bowl. Whisk in the coconut milk, sweetened condensed milk, lime juice, lime zest and salt. The sauce will keep in an airtight container in the refrigerator for up to 1 week.

Extra Credit

● For a party, wow your guests with a batch of **piña coladas** with this as an optional stir-in.

● Blend the sauce with vanilla ice cream and a shot of orange juice for a **shake** that tastes like a Creamsicle on an island vacation.

● Make a tropical **trifle**. Chop up bananas and pineapple. Layer in a clear glass dish with cut-up ladyfingers, whipped cream and drizzles of the lemon grass infusion.

● Dip **shortbread** cookies into the sauce and top with toasted coconut flakes.

Grilled Fruit and Cake Kebabs

Peel and cut 1 ripe but firm mango, ½ peeled and cored pineapple and 4 peeled kiwis into 4cm (1½in) chunks. In a medium bowl, toss the fruit with 2 tablespoons sugar and 2 teaspoons lime zest.

Alternately thread the chunks of fruit and 340g (11¾oz) cubed angel food, Madeira or pound cake (store-bought is fine) onto eight 25cm (10in) skewers. Reserve any excess syrup in the bowl.

Preheat a grill or grill pan over a medium heat. Lightly oil the grill and cook the kebabs, turning occasionally, until grill marks form on all sides, 3–5 minutes total. Transfer to a serving platter. Drizzle any reserved syrup over the skewers. Serve with a ramekin of coconut and lemon grass infusion for dipping. **Serves 4**

Big sections of lemon grass stalks often get discarded because they are too woody and tough to chop. Try making lemon grass tea instead, by steeping them in boiling water until the flavour is released. (This is also a good way to use up leftover fresh ginger.)

BLUEBERRY, LEMON AND THYME COMPOTE

Trivia question: what's the difference between a compote and a coulis? If you said a compote is made of fruit cut into chunks and cooked in a syrup and other flavourings, whereas a coulis usually describes a strained and smooth fruit purée, you're 'berry' correct! (If you enjoyed that, book me for your wedding or corporate event – I'll even come dressed as a berry of your choice.)

Moving on . . . in this recipe, I've gone the compote route, since I love the texture of whole berries within the sauce. (Bonus: you don't have to mess with a strainer.) A hint of fresh thyme and the zing of lemon further livens up the proceedings. Besides using it on sweet things, try this compote as a finishing touch over roast lamb. I know that sounds crazy, but trust me, it's phenomenal.

Makes about 360g (12½oz)

45g (1½oz) sugar
1 teaspoon cornflour
1 teaspoon lemon zest
190g (6½oz) fresh or frozen thawed blueberries
3 sprigs fresh thyme
1 tablespoon fresh lemon juice

1. In a medium saucepan, whisk together the sugar, cornflour, lemon zest and 60ml (2½fl oz) water until the sugar dissolves.

2. Add the blueberries and thyme sprigs. Bring to a simmer over a medium heat and cook until slightly thickened, stirring occasionally, about 8 minutes total. Stir in the lemon juice. Let cool to room temperature and remove the thyme sprigs. Use immediately or store refrigerated in an airtight container for up to 1 week or freeze for up to 3 months.

Extra Credit

● Instead of PB and J, spread a fancy nut butter such as almond or hazelnut on **wholegrain toast** and top with the blueberry, lemon and thyme compote.

● Make a lemon blueberry **Eton mess.** Fold some compote into whipped cream. Add crushed meringue and fold it in. Divide among cups and serve with a sprig of mint.

● Cornbread slices or **corn muffins** left over from dinner? Upcycle them for breakfast the next day by toasting them, spreading with cream cheese or Greek yogurt, then topping with this compote.

● Toss this compote with **sliced peaches** for a fruit salad that puts the canned stuff to shame.

Lemon Ginger Posset

In a medium saucepan, whisk together 100g (3½oz) sugar, 1 teaspoon lemon zest and 2½ teaspoons freshly grated ginger.

Stir in 190ml (6½fl oz) double cream and bring to the boil over a medium-high heat. Continue to boil, stirring occasionally, for about 5 minutes. Remove from the heat and stir in 90ml (6 tablespoons) fresh lemon juice; let cool for 15 minutes.

Stir the cream mixture again and pour it through a fine-mesh sieve into a large measuring cup. Divide the mixture among four ramekins or jars. Refrigerate until set, at least 4 hours or overnight. Serve the posset topped with some blueberry, lemon and thyme compote and a sprig of fresh thyme on each portion. **Serves 4**

SECRET INGREDIENT CARAMEL

When the weather turns cold every year, I get the caramel-making bug. Watching plain sugar transform into such a sublime confection has always fascinated me – it feels like a magic trick. It's a good thing too that I like to watch closely because caramel can go from just right to burnt in a moment. You must remain by the stove with eyes glued on the pot. Like many other people out there, I love salt in my caramel, but I wanted to develop something beyond the ubiquitous sea salt variety. The umami found in miso and soy sauce totally fits the bill. Sounds a bit funky, I know, but just give it a try and you'll see. An added bonus: this sauce makes a great gift presented in a jar to family and friends.

Makes about 550g (1lb 4oz)

225ml (8fl oz) double cream
3 tablespoons sweet white miso
180g (6oz) sugar
85g (3oz) golden or light corn syrup
55g (2oz) unsalted butter, cut into small pieces
1 teaspoon low-sodium soy sauce

1. Warm the cream in a small saucepan over a medium-low heat until hot but not boiling, about 5 minutes. Add the miso and whisk until smooth. Keep warm over a low heat.

2. In a medium saucepan, stir together the sugar, golden syrup and 60ml (4 tablespoons) water. Dip a brush in water and brush it around the rim of the pan to wash away any sugar crystals. Heat over a medium heat without stirring until the sugar has dissolved and becomes a medium amber colour, 12–15 minutes.

3. Whisk in the cream mixture; add gradually as it will bubble up the sides of the saucepan. Cook until slightly thickened, about 3 minutes. With the heat off, whisk in the butter and soy sauce until smooth. Serve warm or room temperature. Store refrigerated in an airtight container for up to 2 weeks. Rewarm in a large bowl over a simmering pot of water.

Extra Credit

- Drizzle cooled caramel over a Madeira or vanilla pound cake, or even **chocolate cake**, or serve a slice of cake in a pool of caramel.

- Draw zigzag lines with a spoonful of caramel over **crêpes**, waffles or pancakes to transform them into an instant dessert.

- Goose up **apple pie** with this caramel sauce for the holidays; the secret ingredient will get the whole table talking.

- **Roast pineapple** rings, place on a serving plate and spoon this sauce into the hole in the middle.

Godzilla Sundae

Place 2 tablespoons of the caramel sauce in the bottom of each of four parfait glasses. Top each with a large scoop of vanilla ice cream drizzled with another tablespoon of caramel. Sprinkle 1 tablespoon dried salted edamame and ¼ teaspoon black sesame seeds on top of the caramel. Then top with 2 tablespoons chopped strawberries.

Repeat with 1 more large scoop of ice cream, more caramel, dried edamame, black sesame seeds and strawberries.

Top with a large dollop of fresh whipped cream and sprinkles of dried salted edamame and sesame seeds. Serve immediately. **Serves 4**

The keys to making a smooth and creamy caramel are a) melting and then b) caramelizing the sugar – without crystals forming at any point. This is why many recipes instruct you to brush the edges of the saucepan with water to remove sugar crystals.

HONEY BEAR NUT SYRUP

Syrupy, nutty and a little spicy, this sauce is inspired by the many flavours of Sicily and its Mediterranean-Arab cuisine, which boasts influences from Italy, Greece, Spain, France and the Middle East. The fennel seeds and orange freshen the palate, while the subtle, rich, nutty flavours of pistachio and sesame add body and crunch. A lot of concentrated flavours are packed into this sauce, so a little goes a long way. The sweet-and-savoury combination works well as a component to a cheese plate or drizzled over grilled fresh figs, peaches and/or apricots.

Makes about 325g (11½oz)

35g (1¼oz) raw unsalted pistachios
35g (1¼oz) raw unsalted almonds
½ teaspoon fennel seeds
1 tablespoon raw sesame seeds
50ml (2fl oz) extra virgin olive oil
6 tablespoons honey
1 teaspoon orange zest
¼ teaspoon sea salt
Pinch of freshly ground black pepper

1. Preheat the oven to 200°C (400°F), Gas Mark 6. Scatter the nuts on a baking sheet and bake for 6–8 minutes, stirring once halfway through, until lightly toasted. Transfer to a board to cool slightly. Finely chop the nuts.

2. Place the fennel seeds and sesame seeds in a small frying pan over a medium heat and stir constantly until toasted, 3–4 minutes. Immediately transfer the seeds to a small bowl.

3. In a medium saucepan, heat the olive oil over a medium heat, about 2 minutes. Add the honey and stir until smooth. Add the reserved nuts and seeds and stir to combine and heat through. Stir in the orange zest, salt and black pepper. Serve warm or room temperature. Store in an airtight container at room temperature for up to 1 week. Stir well before using the sauce, as the ingredients separate overnight.

Extra Credit

● Grill a piece of anadama, banana or **courgette (zucchini) bread**, then spread with crème fraîche and drizzle with the honey nut syrup.

● Add mustard and vinegar to the sauce to make a salad dressing – works especially well with spicy, nutty greens or **chicories** (e.g., rocket (arugula), spinach, dandelion greens or radicchio).

Sticky Bread Knots

Preheat the oven to 240°C (475°F), Gas Mark 9. Divide 450g (1lb) pizza dough into 12 pieces and roll each piece into a 15cm (6in) rope. Form each into a knot by crossing the rope ends, leaving a hole in the centre. Bring the end that lies on top up through the bottom of the hole. You may have to tug on the end a bit to get it to come through.

Place the knots 5cm (2in) apart on a parchment-lined baking sheet. Brush each with olive oil and sprinkle with salt. Bake until golden brown on top, 12–14 minutes.

Place the honey bear nut syrup in a shallow bowl. When the knots are done, transfer the paper, with the knots, to a surface. Immediately roll each knot in the honey syrup to coat and spoon some additional nuts and sauce over the top. Allow to cool and firm up. Serve warm or room temperature. **Makes 12**

● Use as a glaze for steamed, mashed, or roasted carrots, **parsnips**, turnips or swede.

● Serve **steel-cut oats** with almond milk, dried cranberries and a drizzle of this syrup.

Sauce-Making Tools

In my cooking classes, I occasionally get asked about what tools and supplies I would recommend when setting up a home kitchen. I could go on and on about this, but for the purposes of this book let me stick with sauces. The following are my go-to devices and tools for sauce-making.

High-Powered Blender

After having gone through many blenders over the years I am convinced that investing in a good one will save you money in the long run. Even the mid-priced ones tend to break down. The high-powered blenders, on the other hand, are workhorses that can take a good beating (no pun intended). A high-powered blender also yields the most velvety sauce. Make sure your blender has a clear jug; you need to be able to see the texture of your mixture to know when you've reached the desired consistency.

Stick Blender

While it won't achieve quite the same smoothness as a high-powered blender, a stick blender is a good option if you are making large quantities of sauce in a heavy pot or blended soups. They are generally easier to clean and take up less space – both definite bonuses.

Food Processor

For chopping and coarsely blending ingredients, nothing beats a food processor. It gives you more control than a blender; the pulse function is especially useful for this purpose. I also love that you can clean most food processor parts in a dishwasher.

Mortar and Pestle

It's physically more work, but grinding spices and herbs by hand with a mortar and pestle not only allows you to release their fragrant oils but also gives you total control over the grind. (Plus they look so pretty on the work surface. You can collect beautiful specimens from around the world: volcanic stone from Mexico, marble from Italy, olive wood from Spain.)

Fine-Mesh Strainer

I can't say enough good things about these tools. I've used them to help get optimal smoothness in so many mixtures – including getting lumps, seeds and citrus peel out of sauces. If your sauce is thick and won't strain easily, using a rubber spatula to push it through the fine mesh usually does the trick.

Rubber Spatula

The silicone variety is dishwasher safe and great for getting into the corners of a saucepan that a wooden or metal spoon can't reach. Use them to scrape every last bit of sauce out of the saucepan or bowl and into the serving dish.

Large Wooden and Metal Spoons

Use heavy wooden spoons when making creamy sauces such as the Katia's Creamy Vanilla Elixir (page 154) since they are thicker than a metal spoon and can really smooth and stir the thick sauce. I prefer metal spoons for sauces that are quite hot in temperature and thinner in texture.

Heavy-Bottomed Pots and Pans

Good-quality pots and pans are always wise investments. The heavy bottoms help with even heating. The ones I use are stainless steel. For sauce-making purposes I recommend having on hand a small saucepan, medium saucepan, large saucepan and a large high-sided frying pan.

Casserole

This is great when making a larger batch of sauce. I like how the mixture heats up slowly and evenly.

Cast-Iron Frying Pan

I got rid of my nonstick pans years ago and don't miss them at all. My seasoned cast iron frying pan has replaced the need for nonstick. Cooking on it feels so much safer, plus it wasn't too expensive and will last a lifetime. Just make sure you keep the surface well seasoned. I tend to use soap very sparingly on these pans – only when really needed. Normally all they need is a good scrub with coarse salt and water. After cleaning, place the wet pan back over the heat until dry, then use kitchen paper or rag to rub with a thin coating of a neutral oil such as rapeseed.

Cast-Iron Stovetop Grill

We sometimes grill outside in the winter, but that's not always fun in Maine. When feeling less ambitious we take it indoors with this handy pan. A cast-iron stovetop grill allows you to make some of the grilled sauces such as the Artichoke and Lemon Tapenade (page 142) and the Aubergine Zhoug (page 120) inside. Clean and season the grill pan the same way you would a cast-iron frying pan (see opposite).

Microplane

These tools work like a box grater, but are way less bulky and can fit in the drawer. Consequently I have them in every shape and size. I use them for grating cheese, citrus peel, chocolate, cinnamon and nutmeg.

Reamer or Citrus Juicer

If you use a lot of fresh citrus in your cooking, a good reamer or citrus juicer is a must. You can always use your hands to squeeze the fresh fruit, but on the East Coast of the US, where citrus is pricier, you want to make sure to get every last drop of juice out of the fruit.

Whisk

A good stainless-steel whisk smooths out and lightens the texture of sauces. It's the classic symbol of a saucier, and for good reason.

Acknowledgements

Developing, writing and styling the recipes for this book has been a thrill. It also has been a massive undertaking that truly took a village to accomplish. I would like to give my thanks to the following:

First and foremost, to my wonderful family and friends for their patience, love, feedback and encouragement throughout this process.

To my husband, Jon, for your love and endless support, for making me laugh, and for your keen editorial eye and unpaid late night/early morning editing.

To my Relish&Co. friends and partners, Stacey Cramp and Jennifer S. Muller, for your fabulous visual/design sense and talent. Not a day goes by that I don't feel grateful and lucky that we found each other and get to work together.

To Kyle Books for giving me this extraordinary opportunity.

To Chris Steighner, editor, for your advice, ideas and superb editing skills. And to Sarah Scheffel, whose copyedits greatly improved the text throughout.

To Heather Noonan-Kelly, whose photo-editing talent and on-set assistance with both photos and food prep made our shoots run more smoothly.

To all the recipe testers, whose feedback helped me tweak, refine and improve these sauces and dishes: Gillian Kitchings, Moire Madden, Linda Christman, Melissa Lacasse and to my two Relish&Co. partners.

Thank you to Anwar and Shaymaa Jailawi for your invaluable childcare help, friendship and feedback as recipe tasters.

To the Institute of Culinary Education for the skills, techniques and knowledge that laid the foundation of my culinary journey, and to all the teachers, mentors and colleagues I've learned from along the way.

About the Author

Vanessa Seder is a chef, food stylist, teacher and a founding member of Relish&Co., a culinary design collaborative based in Portland, Maine. A graduate of the Institute of Culinary Education, Vanessa has developed recipes for *Ladies Home Journal*, *Real Simple*, *All You*, *Health*, *Cooking Light* and Hannaford's *Fresh*. Previously an associate food editor at *Ladies Home Journal*, Vanessa has also worked as a food stylist for television, video, magazines and books, as well as for national brands. She is also a regular culinary instructor at the Stonewall Kitchen headquarters in York, Maine.